The

Kama Sutra of Celibacy:

101 Ways to be Successfully Celibate

This book is designed for adult readers.
Please look for the teen version to be released soon.

by

The Lady M

(Formerly C. L. Summers)

The Kama Sutra of Celibacy: 101 Ways to be Successfully Celibate
Copyright © 2011 by C. L. Summers
Published by A Yellow Butterfly Ventures
Gallatin, TN 37066
http://www.KamaSutraofCelibacy.com

ISBN-13: 978-0615547329
ISBN-10: 061554732X

For Worldwide Distribution, Printed in the U.S.A.

I dedicate this book to all who choose to honor their heart, mind, soul, and body through walking the path of celibacy. You are not alone in this journey. There are others out there who are willing to wait with, and for you until marriage. Don't sacrifice yourself for someone who isn't willing to wait!

Table of Contents

Introduction

I offer this book as a guide to help you be successful in your walk of celibacy. I don't proclaim to be an expert or a great saint. What I am is a woman who has and continues to walk the path that you are now embarking upon. I share my experiences as my open testimony to support and encourage you to help you to meet your goal of celibacy.

Celibacy is not just a physical surrender; it is also mental, emotional and spiritual in nature. Because this is the case, we must address each of these facets when we arm ourselves for the task of living a life of celibacy. For this reason, we talk about each of these areas in this book. We can't take celibacy, place it in a box, and put it up on a shelf, only to pull it out when we have an itch that we fear scratching. It's good to pull it out at that time, but it's great to keep it with you on a daily basis. Just as we need air, water, food and sleep daily, we must also acknowledge our sexual wants and desires daily. It doesn't mean that we act on them, but that we acknowledge that they are there so we can learn how to control them, whatever that desire is. And let's be real here. If you watch television, listen to music, read a book, drive or walk down a street, you will encounter something or someone with the potential to arouse some sense of sexual desire in you.

Okay, so let's take all the enticers away. Say you're a hermit living without books, television, phone and no method of getting any information from the outside world. Let's say I give you that option (highly unlikely, but I'll give it to you). You still have hormones raging through your body that crave to be fulfilled.

Think about a baby. An infant doesn't know what milk or food is, but when their body begins to crave it, *you will* certainly know it. If you take too long to feed that baby, everyone in the near vicinity will know that that child has a need that needs to be met. If you're the parent of that child they will be looking to you to help meet the needs of that crying child, as soon as possible. The same is true with our sexual desires. And for that reason, we must be mindful in how we deal with managing those desires.

So why do we need a book to help us on this journey of celibacy? Why do we even have to talk about it? We're adults. We know how to conduct ourselves. We can simply make the choice to be celibate and move on with it, right? Wrong! It is not that simple. Sexual desires impact us every day of our lives whether we want them to or not. If we are not in control of our thoughts and feelings in this area of our lives, we are more susceptible to falling victim to our own will, instead of the will of God. We must guard our mind, our heart, our ears and our surroundings so we can control what enters our soul, our heart and our minds. The less we allow in the less we have to deal with on a daily basis.

Let's look at it from a different approach. In the third year of his first term, (at the time this book was written), America's first black president, Barack Obama, was virtually scandal-free. The most people tried to say about him was that he wasn't born in this country. They saw his birth certificate detailing his place of birth, and yet they still tried to challenge it because there was nothing else for them to challenge or impeach him on. As far as anyone could tell at the time, President Obama's record was squeaky-clean, save for the weed he smoked in college, which he already told us about in his books.

So why hadn't we heard anything about Obama at this point? It's because once he made the decision that he wanted to be president many years ago, he held to his goal of one day occupying the White House. From that moment on, the future Commander-in-Chief began guarding his heart, his mind, his ears, his confidants and his environment. He did this because he didn't want to have something negative from his past resurface, one day down the line, and jeopardize his chances of him reaching his ultimate goal.

Another strategic move Obama made was to recruit an army of supporters to help him with his goal. He spoke to everyone about what he wanted to do and where he wanted to go. He believed in who he was, what he was doing and made everyone he encountered believe in his goal, supporters and non-supporters alike. Everyone knew of his goal and they either helped him or tried to hinder him in achieving it. The beauty of sharing his goal with supporters and non-supporters is that Obama then knew how to interact with each of those groups.

Obama knew what limitations to place on some and how much access to grant to others. He was successful in winning his run to the White House, in part, because he constantly kept his goal before him. He spoke on it and acted on it daily. He recruited soldiers to build his army, and established his limitations and mode of operation with those against him. These are some of the same principles that you'll read about in each of the four sections of this book to help you have a successful walk of celibacy.

Another example of someone who followed a standard of living and saw it pay off greatly in her life is media mogul Oprah Winfrey. She has guarded herself and surrounded herself with people who would support and encourage her. Winfrey limited her time with those looking to derail her or meant her harm. It's because of that fierce mindset and determination that she is one of the most revered women in modern history.

* * * * *

As you progress through this book, pay attention to words that are underlined. They are "survival" words to guide you in your reading. These key survival words are action or focus words to help you zero in on the idea or lesson of the topic that you are reading. Don't be a passive reader of these words. Instead, be an active reader and doer. These words will be salt beneath your feet when the road gets slippery. They will serve as your light at the end of the tunnel. So pay attention and hold them close. For now I will begin with a short list of words to get you started. As more survival words begin to speak to you through your walk with God, add them to the list and carry them with you each day. These words will become part of your testimony as you help others reach the journey that you have just begun!

Faith, Courage, Worthy/Worthwhile, Strength, Promise, Support
Forgiveness, Goal, Commitment, Love, Yes
(and all too important) NO!

Words of Encouragement

There is one very important reminder that I must give you that seems obvious but still needs to be stated. It is so critically important that you get this, as it will propel you forward in your walk. Following your relationship and belief in God, you must love and embrace You! Know and understand your value to you, to God and to the world as a whole. Know who You are! You are a child of God. If you don't fully and completely love and embrace You, your journey will be that much harder. By loving and embracing You, You will want, seek and desire nothing but the best for You. Wanting the best for You is wanting all that God wants and has for You, and to be pleasing in the eyesight of the Father who loves You dearly. You obtain and achieve His favor with your love and obedience to Him. But if You can't fully love and embrace You, how can You truly love and obey the Father? It all starts with love.

This realization came to me after watching pre-concert footage of pop star Lady Gaga in her dressing room right before a show at Madison Square Garden. She is a multi-millionaire and a mega superstar many times over with an uncountable fan base, or "Little Monsters" as she calls them. Yet, with all of her success and fame, Gaga, in that video, still sees herself as a failure and a skinny, little high school girl wanting and lacking love. What this revealed to me was that no matter what heights of fame she achieves, she would always feel that way until she learns to truly love and embrace herself. Until she learns to appreciate herself for who she is, she will always fall short of the mark in her own eyes. Therefore, she will always struggle to reach her goals, even when she has surpassed them in the eyes of the world.

The journey that you are embarking on is a great and difficult one. Don't make it any harder for yourself by forgetting to start with one of the most basic and crucial building blocks of loving and embracing You!

So roll up your sleeves, take notes, recruit your army and get to work!

<u>Note:</u> From time to time you will see "we" being used, don't be confused. The "we" is God and myself, as He is speaking through me in many of the words that I write. I alone am not enough to provide guidance in this work!

How to Use This Book

The Kama Sutra of Celibacy: 101 Ways to be Successfully Celibate is not your ordinary book, but you probably already figured that out. It is no accident that you are reading this book. Something in your spirit and heart has drawn you to these pages. That spirit is God. He knew that you were struggling in this area and has sent this book especially for you. Yes, *You*! The devil wants you to believe that you are not strong enough to take on this journey and succeed. But God says, *yes you are* and has sent His word to guide you through this process.

Please take heed when reading this book as there is a formula laid out to guide you through each step and to set you on the path of success. The formula is easy. All you have to do is to read this book in order, pray, have faith, meditate on the words found in these pages and put them into action. That's it. It's that simple!

I know with this book being laid out in 101 ways you will be tempted to jump around at random in your reading. You can get helpful tips by doing so, but you are not accessing the full power of this book if you do that. The book was initially designed to be shared in four parts, but was combined into one to ensure that you get the full breadth of all of its parts. Each section is designed as a building block upon the previous section in the same way that God instructs us to put on the full suit of armor.

Therefore, put on every piece of God's armor so you will be able to resist the enemy in the time of evil. Then after the battle you will still be standing firm. Stand your ground, putting on the belt of truth and the body armor of God's righteousness. For shoes, put on the peace that comes from the Good News so that you will be fully prepared. In addition to all of these, hold up the shield of faith to stop the fiery arrows of the devil. Put on salvation as your helmet, and take the sword of the Spirit, which is the word of God.

-Ephesians 6:13-17 (NLT)

Be cautioned, this book is not as effective read in parts as it is as a whole. Just as Rick Warren's book *The Purpose Driven® Life* was best read and followed by going in the order of the 40 days, so is this book. Each step builds on the last step. First you must start with learning the foundation (Section I), the ground rules. Then you must learn what it is like for men and women to live as a single celibate (Sections II and III). Finally, once you have gained all that knowledge, you are now ready to move forward in celibacy as a celibate couple (Section IV).

Don't cheat yourself or your current or future partner by not putting in the work. You can't become a senior in high school or college by not first being a freshman, sophomore, and a junior first. Follow the steps and you will complete your journey and graduate with success!

SECTION I

Laying the Foundation for the Work Ahead

1: Trust in <u>God</u>

Know that He has got your back and won't ever give you more than you can handle. He will always provide you with a way out or guidance in every situation that you face. When it seems that your task is insurmountable, you have a secret weapon that you can call on at any time regardless of where you are and who is around. That weapon is the name of Jesus, who is the Son of God. There is great and tremendous power in that name and it can bind your enemies on the spot! I have done it and seen it for myself. So I know it works!

I had an incident once where someone was yelling at me. Then I remembered that calling on the name of Jesus can and will stop him in his tracks. As he spoke, I called the name Jesus in my head, over and over again and that person began stumbling and fumbling all over his words. He then became so frustrated that his only course of action was to just shut up! I didn't have to do a thing other than call on Jesus' name and the attack stopped instantly. The only thing left for him to do was to walk away from me. That man had no clue what had just happened to him. Use this weapon when you are in a situation that you don't know how to get out of, or when faced with someone who doesn't seem to understand the word "NO!" It is so simple and yet so powerful. It is but one small example of how trusting in God can see you through and how He can provide a way out of any situation!

When you don't know which way to go or what to do, STOP. Take a breath and remember that God will direct your path in the right direction if you allow Him to do so. Trust Him to take over the reins, and then let go.

2: Have <u>Faith</u> That You Will Achieve Your Goal, with God's Help

We can't do it alone! God is there to help us. He wants us to turn to Him for help in everything that we do. This is why He is always available to us day or night. If we are aligning ourselves with His word, then He is faithful to help us achieve it.

Seek the Kingdom of God above all else, and live righteously, and he will give you everything you need.

–Matthew 6:33 (NLT)

God wants to help us succeed in life, but we need to have faith in Him; that He will do what He has promised in His Word. If you believe that you can do it, then you can. If you do not believe, you may as well stop reading now as nothing else I say can or will help you if you don't have faith that you will be successful in this area.

3: Say *"Yes"* to You and the Goal You've Set for Yourself

"Yes, I can do it! Yes, I will make it through to the end! Yes, I am worth it. Yes, I am worth the wait!" At the beginning of this book we talked about loving and embracing yourself. Part of loving and embracing You is saying, "Yes, I am worth the wait!" If you don't first believe, no one else will believe. Saying, "yes" to you will ward off those who don't want to see you succeed. Believe me they are out there. And if this doesn't ward them off, identify them as people who are not worthy to go with you on this journey. Move on without them.

4: **Prepare** Your Mind for the Mental Battle

The battle will not be physical alone. Remember, wars are lost in the mind before a foot ever touches a grain of sand. The children of Israel are a perfect example of how not preparing your mind for the battle ahead can cause you to be unsuccessful in obtaining your goal. God promised them that He would take them to the Promised Land. But instead of just trusting in His word, they made it up in their minds that the giants who resided in that land were too strong for them to face, even though God had already promised them victory (Numbers 13: 30-33).

Know why you're doing this and what your expected goal is before you start this journey. You will need to keep this in front of you every step of the way! Be ready, your mind may play tricks on you and develop clever schemes and tactics to persuade you that you don't need to be celibate or at the very least, not celibate 100% of the

---

time. Don't be fooled. It is just a trick from the devil to get you to turn to his way of doing things, instead of God's way.

5: Keep Forgiveness in Your Front Pocket

You will need it! You may not be as successful as you'd like to be in the beginning, in the middle or even towards the end of your walk. But should you fail, forgive yourself and ask God to forgive you and He will. He will also wipe away your tears and wash the slate clean.

For me, the first six months can be a bit difficult starting out. But after that, it's pretty much smooth sailing from there - until I hit the next hill! One of my favorite songs is titled "I Try," by singing duo Mary Mary. The song talks about what happens when we try to do things in our own strength instead of God's strength. It talks about how we can get back on the right path, with God's help. I've turned to this song many times for encouragement during the times I have not been as strong, or as successful as I'd like to be on this journey. It talks about God's forgiveness and His granting of another chance. It talks about learning to let go of your mistakes and moving forward afresh, with God.

Grasping this step is critically important because of the direction in which it can take you. Whenever I failed in meeting the standards I set for myself, I'd spend days in sorrow and regret for what I had done and I couldn't move forward until I got over it, eventually. That is why I love this song so, because it speaks the truth. At some point we are all going to fail in some area of our life. We are human. If not in the walk of celibacy, in the area of being a good friend or whatever area we desire to do right. No matter how hard we try, it will occur. But the beauty is that God is there to catch us, pick us up and take us to the next step, stronger than we were before we fell.

Once we ask God for His forgiveness (with a sincere heart), He gives it to us. So if God is able to forgive you and throw your sins into the depths of the sea (Micah 7:18-19.), then who are we to hold onto the guilt of the sin? Forgive yourself and don't let the devil allow you to punish yourself for something that your Heavenly Father has already absolved of you. Forgive yourself, learn from it and move on with the lesson learned in hand for the next battle.

6: Keep "<u>NO</u>" on a Chain around Your Neck

Old friends, lovers and those you wanted to get with or "try out," but couldn't or never thought you would have the opportunity with, can (and some will) find your number or run into you while at the grocery store or some other random place. Satan loves to get in your way when you're working for and with God. But our Father has armed us with a mighty tool: "NO," "NO THANKS," "NO, I'LL PASS!"

But God doesn't just stop there. He'll also provide you with an escape route to get you out of there after you've struck and clubbed them with your mighty weapon of "**NO!**"

7: Fill Your <u>Toolbox</u> for the Battle

Tools of the trade include, but are not limited to:

- A good Bible (A One-Year Bible can be very helpful. No matter what any given day brings, the assigned readings for that day always has a word to give me solace.)
- A few gospel CDs (I love Mary Mary, always a great song to be found!)
- The Bible Promise Book (I have my friend "Tanya" to thank for mine!)
- A prayer closet (A space for you and Jesus to talk uninterrupted.)
- A Christian mentor/friend to talk things through and to remind you of your goals when you sometimes want to forget.
- Bible verse websites or phone applications – YouVersion.com (this app also includes reading plans BibleInfo.com, Bibletools.org and BibleGateway.com are good ones. (On my iPhone I have Just 1 Word/Bible +1 app. With this app I am able to go to a specific book and verse and read it in one version or with a click or two, switch to many other versions of the Bible for that same scripture.)

There are other Bible apps that you can find that will meet your needs and many are free. Find one that you like and load it onto your smart phone so it's available anywhere or anytime you need it.

8: <u>Recruit</u> Soldiers in Your Army (Tell Others of Your Goal)

So many times we tell our friends and family our goals to lose weight, stop smoking, or to exercise more. They're our faithful watch guards to tell us to "put the brownie down and back away from the table." Or they give us those dirty looks when a cigarette is lit followed by "I thought you were trying to quit!" God sends those same friends to help you with your celibacy goals as well. My most loyal friend and soldier in this area was the one time love of my life. My hormones would say yes and he would say **No!** Mostly because he knew what I was striving to achieve. He wouldn't let me mistreat myself or betray my spirit by listening to my hormones.

People have told me that I shouldn't tell others that I'm celibate and have been for x amount of years, because it's none of their business. But by telling others, I'm ensuring that I'm not alone in this battle. I am, in fact, recruiting my army and identifying my enemies (non-supporters) all at once. Remember that iron sharpens iron. In addition to helping advance my own personal goal of celibacy, I am also telling others that they too can do it. I've become a living example of someone they know who is successful in this journey. Without even knowing it, speaking on what you're doing could be an encouragement to someone else to turn six days or six weeks into six months or longer!

Don't be ashamed of what you're doing. I wear my celibacy as a badge of honor. I tote it around just as I would a new Fendi or Coach™ purse! As an added bonus, He (God) helps us weed out some people who don't need to be in the picture; those wanting to help you "get over" this little problem of celibacy you have, as they like to think of it. As you make strides along your journey, you'll notice those who tried to obstruct your path will be forced to take a step in the other direction when you let them know who you are up front, and what you're doing. But don't think all will walk away. Some will try to break the streak. For the would-be streak breakers, say a prayer and keep it moving. Let God handle them!

9: **Know <u>Your Value</u>**

You are worthwhile and therefore, *worth the wait*! Think how special you'd feel to meet your soul mate and learn that they have removed themselves from the world's bed to only lay in the marital bed with you! Aside from being a virgin, what better gift can you give your spouse other than being a born again virgin? Sex is a gift to marriage. Give that gift to your spouse. You accomplish this by knowing your worth, your value!

10: **<u>Get Ready</u> for the Journey**

Make the decision and the commitment to achieve your goal of celibacy, one day at a time. Prepare yourself mentally, emotionally and environmentally and review those you spend your time with. Some of those people may need to go! If they are not supporting you in your goal, then they are a potential threat to your success. If they are, limit your time with them or remove them from your life completely!

* * * * *

Steps one through ten are to be used as a foundation, suiting up for the journey ahead. The real work begins now. It is filled with many rewards along the way. But just as there are rewards, there are also hurdles and puddles along the path. In a city where there is construction, there will also be detours to route traffic around it to continue a smooth flow. The same is true with God, as He will always set up detours and special routes designed to make a way out of, or around the trouble. Sometimes the way out will be physical. Sometimes the way will be mental or emotional (leaving you in the physical realm of the trouble, but relieving the mind and diminishing the desire so that it has little to no impact on you). Whatever method He chooses to use, know that He will be there to assist you in being successful in your walk of celibacy. You only need to ask Him for His help. If you're too weak to speak, just lean on God.

Be sure that your tools are in place and that your army is ready for the battle. The work is just beginning. There will be some easy days and some rough days, but ultimately your reward lies in Heaven when the Father says, *"Well done, Thy good and faithful servant."* (Matthew 25:21). Remember that you're not alone! There are many others, men and women, along with the Heavenly Father that are taking this journey with you. **Time to begin!**

11: Make the <u>Decision</u> to Live for God and Not for Self

Know why you're making the choice to be celibate and whom your choice is for. You'd hate to make the choice to be celibate in exchange for finding or waiting for your spouse to come, only to find that you are better suited to singlehood.

I wish that all men were like I myself am [in this matter of self-control]. But each has his own special gift from God, one of this kind and one of another. But to the unmarried people and to the widows, I declare that it is well (good, advantageous, expedient, and wholesome) for them to remain [single] even as I do.

–1 Corinthians 7:7-8 (AMP)

If late in life you find this to be true (that you were better suited for singlehood), and the only reason you were celibate was for a form of exchange for getting a spouse, you will be devastated with your choice and will feel that you have cheated yourself. No one wants to go through life feeling like they've cheated themselves. When you make the decision, it should be one of wanting to please God, not to get something out of the deal. It has to be all for God and self-preservation, or not at all.

12: <u>Last Time</u> is the Last Time

This doesn't mean that you go and have a "last time." It means whenever it was that you last had sex, that *is* the last time. Don't get caught up in the myth that now that you're starting your journey of celibacy that you have to have one for the road. If it's bad, you'll want to go back and make sure "the last time" is good. That way you can have something to hold on to during the times you're awaiting God to bring your celibacy to an end through marriage. If it's good, you'll long for more of it. You'll convince yourself that you need more of it and that your body deserves it. If you don't let the last time *be* the last time, where will you draw the line?

13: Start Fresh <u>Daily</u>

Which is easier, planning the next 730 days (two years) of your life in advance, or waking up each day and planning that day? Of course one day at a time is easier. You never know what each day will bring to you, good or bad. If you plan it all out and write it down, you open yourself up to others being able to come in and alter your plans. You are essentially an open book for others to write their will for you and your life into your days' plans. But if you start each day fresh and ask God to be your guide and to direct your path, to order your steps in His will, your days' plans are only between you and God. By doing this you are making it harder for others to influence your plans. This journey only has to be as hard as you want or make it to be. Whatever happened yesterday, *happened yesterday*. It doesn't have to impact what you do today.

This was hard for me to learn. You could always tell when I fell short of my goal. The days following a sexual encounter, I would be upset, depressed and beat myself up until I could no longer take it. Then, somehow (through prayer), I would pull myself together and get back on track again. During this time, I wasted a lot of time that could have been spent giving honor to God and living in His obedience. By carrying yesterday into today, I robbed God of time with Him and gave Satan time and power over my life when God had already forgiven me when I first asked Him to. When we mess up, we should repent, forgive ourselves and move on in obedience. Give yourself time to grieve if you need to, but set a time limit on grieving for 10 minutes, 30 at most. Then let it go and move on! When you lay down to sleep that night, lay down that burden and be certain not to pick it up the next morning, or ever again. It is the only way you will be able to keep stepping toward God!

On my cell phone I have a daily alarm titled, "Wake Up! It's a New Day!" If you messed up yesterday, say a prayer and ask God to show you where you went wrong and a new route to get around that roadblock the next time you come across it. Then move on! If yesterday was a great day, build on it and keep it movin'. If it wasn't, let it go and keep it going. The ultimate goal is to keep moving in a direction that honors and pleases God, each day!

14: Let <u>Temptation</u> Make You, Not Break You

Sometimes temptation gets so hectic that it seems easier to just give in to it than to fight it. Guess what? You've guessed it; it's a lie straight from hell! God will always open a window, unseal a crack or expose a cubbyhole for you to slip out of (physically, mentally or emotionally). Once you're on the other side you'll be better able to spot it when it comes around again and walk on by, instead of walking into temptation's welcoming doorway.

Learn what areas tempt you the most and make every attempt to avoid them in the future. If you know it's a certain song that winds you up, remove it from your library or change the station. When you know what sets you off and you avoid it, you've just achieved a victory. Knowledge of that victory will help propel you through your next test successfully.

15: Know Your <u>Triggers</u>, Your Five Senses

Your triggers can be related to your five senses (touch, taste, sound, smell and sight). They can also be people, places and things. One of my major triggers was a friend we'll call "Phillip" for this book. All he had to do was to enter into my presence (physically or mentally, it didn't matter). He didn't have to speak, touch me or even look at me, and I was in trouble. But thank God he was one of the soldiers in my army and I must say he was definitely a general! He kept me strong and fighting when I wanted to give in to my body's desires. He reminded me of my goal and resisted my attempts to persuade him into following what my body said I wanted, versus what my spirit wanted. But I wouldn't recommend that you try that with *anyone*.

I was blessed to have someone like him in my life. Even though he served as my strength most of the time, he was also still a man and sometimes the man would present himself to me. It was in those moments when I had to decide if I really wanted to remain celibate or not. I would have to stop and think hard and make a decision, in a matter of seconds (as by that time he was heated). Thank God he was a man of honor, always!

16: **Learn Your Triggers** – <u>Smell</u>

Like so many things, a scent can be a trigger to remind you of times past and make you want to revisit them. Enjoy the scents of past lives but don't linger in them. There are plenty of new scents to smell, scents that will soothe your soul, not make it cry from regret.

17: **Learn Your Triggers** – <u>Taste</u>

It could be a favorite drink, alcoholic or non-alcoholic; a dessert that the other loves; or the way they always tasted when you kissed them. Taste can be a trigger if you allow it to be. So often we associate food with emotions. But remember food is food and emotion is emotion. Don't let one take you some place that you've just left or are struggling to escape from.

18: **Learn Your Triggers** – <u>Sound</u>

Music is a major trigger for me. It seems that at least one song is attached to one past lover or another. There were some songs I was not able to listen to without being transported back to those moments of ecstasy. If I wanted to keep a certain song in my repertoire, I had to learn to disassociate any past memories or feeling from it. If I couldn't, I hit the delete button. But it doesn't have to be a song. Words of a lost love can be heard in dreams, in poems or any vessel that delivers sound. Sound can even have the power to make you think they're actually there with you. But don't be fooled. Triggers are designed to make you reminisce on times of the past. They also try to convince you that maybe those times shouldn't remain in the past, and that celibacy is not the way to go. Don't believe it. It's a lie straight from hell. Fill your ears with the words of God, and songs of praise and you'll turn a trigger into a tool.

19: **Learn Your Triggers – Sight**

Sight can be a powerful trigger without one even realizing its power. Back in my early 20s, prior to becoming celibate, there was a man who I was involved with. The nature of our relationship was strictly maintenance. We never went out and only met at his house. The experiences I had with this man were some of the best of my life and I was certainly hooked. So much so that this man became my kryptonite.

Many years later, I could still be momentarily stalled when I saw this man in person, or even in a picture. My breath would catch in my chest and my body would tingle. I have absolutely no desire for this man at this point in my life, nor will I in the future. But the sight of him triggered something in me. Through the grace of God, I was aware of this trigger and was able to quickly dismiss it and not allow it to linger and develop into something more. Be mindful of the things that you allow to enter your line of sight.

20: **Learn Your Triggers – Touch**

Touch can be a funny thing, especially by the wrong person. Back in high school, I remember being on the bus, sitting on my knees facing the back of the seat, looking over the seat behind me. A guy I knew stroked the back of my leg behind my knee and it sent shivers up my spine. The touch was as light as air, but held enough weight to bring about a strong reaction in me in an area that I knew nothing of.

Touch doesn't have to be deliberate in its delivery; it can happen by mere accident. But it can send you on a whirlwind of desire and transport you to a place you thought you left behind. As we're being careful with the things that we allow into our minds, we also must be careful with what touches us in general, and what emotions they can stir up.

21: **Learn Your Triggers – Memories**

Sometimes when we're lonely or bored we think about things and people from our past. Sometimes if we close our eyes and let out minds wander a bit, we can transport ourselves through those sweet memories back to a time that we once knew. Scent kicks in and we can sometimes remember the way the other person smelled. If you allow yourself to get caught up enough in the thought, you can almost feel the touch or the sensations you experienced when you were last with that person, especially if it's someone you loved. But be careful, these kinds of thoughts can be very dangerous. They can make you rationalize and question your current path of celibacy.

Many times when dwelling on memories we tend to remember most of the good and less of the bad. We glamorize the good parts and make excuses for the rest. We all know how nice it is to visit with an old friend and think that because we do it in the mind, that it's harmless. But think of it as a type of vacation. At some point you need to pack it up and go home. At some point you need to pack up those memories and return to the present. When memories surface, and they will, smile and leave them where they are…in the past. You are the only one who has control over your mind, so take control of your thoughts and your memories. It won't happen instantly, but with practice it can and will happen. I try to remember what Paul said about living in the past and the present.

Brethren, I do not count myself to have apprehended; but one thing I do, forgetting those things which are behind and reaching forward to those things which are ahead, I press toward the goal for the prize of the upward call of God in Christ Jesus.

–Philippians 3:13-14

22: Learn Your Triggers – <u>People, Places and Things</u>

For some, sex outside of marriage can be just as much of an addiction as any other sin or drug that we allow to come into our lives. You have to want to be celibate in your singlehood just as a drug addict and alcoholic has to want to be free of drugs and alcohol. There are some people you just can't hang around anymore if you desire to change. If there is someone who you've been intimate with and/or knows your triggers, you need to limit or discontinue your contact with them. Sometimes it's as easy as just not going to certain places, listening to certain songs or talking about certain subjects with them. If there is a favorite article of clothing that you always wore or habit you participated in when you weren't practicing celibacy, get rid of it. Let it go. Donate it, throw it away or learn a new habit.

When it came to Philip, I had to keep myself from going over to his house, especially in his bedroom where a lot of times we just hung out there watching TV. With others I just had to not return their calls or keep walking when I ran into them. It's funny how you can know where someone will be without even realizing it; events that will bring him or her out along with the possible opportunity that you may be able to spend time with him or her. Then there are those people who try to encourage you that there's nothing wrong with having a little fun, that your body deserves it. But those are the ones who care nothing about your soul. It is wise to stay away from those people as well.

23: **Surround Yourself with <u>Like Minds</u>**

As iron sharpens iron, So a man sharpens the countenance of his friend.

–Proverbs 27:17

This celibacy walk will at times be no picnic, this I can guarantee you. But we do it so we can be pleasing in the sight of God. The second half of Proverbs 27:18 gives us proof of this.

…So he who waits on his master will be honored.

–Proverbs 27:18

It's not enough to just have people in your corner who believe in what you're doing for yourself. You also need those who believe in it for themselves. A person who is not on the walk of celibacy cannot encourage you to remain faithful to your goal when they are doing the exact opposite. How much value and weight will you place on their words when you know that they don't live by those words? How willing are you to read this book if I was a virgin and never personally experienced the pangs of sexual withdrawal? Probably not much! You have to live the example before you can be the example. Being the example gives you your testimony to help others on the same path.

As friends we share our lives and experiences with those we hold dear and close to us. If you are trying not to drink or spend unnecessary money, how helpful is it to be with someone who is telling you about some great new drink they've found or made, or the latest greatest fashions and gadgets that they just bought? You may be strong for a while, but at some point you'll want to try that new liquor or buy what they have so you are not feeling left out. It's the same thing with sex. You remember how good you thought it was, even if it wasn't all that great. You'll briefly forget how detached you felt the last time you were in that position, and couldn't wait until it was over because you knew you were betraying your God and your soul by being there.

Christian singles ministries are a good place to meet like-minded individuals. If the church that you attend doesn't currently have one, talk to your pastor about starting one. Reach out to singles ministries at other churches in the meantime to see what they are doing to help you get started. Christian bookstores are another source for getting you started as they have books to help you start a singles ministry. If you don't want to do it through a church, start your own group of celibate singles. You can even create a MeetUp® group where you can have face-to-face outings to exchange best practices and have activities that provide you with an outlet. However you do it, make sure that it works for you and that you can benefit from it. Think of it as another tool in your toolbox!

24: <u>Clean</u> Out Your House

Sexy lingerie, videos, toys, literature (and I use the word loosely), and special songs that tell you it's okay, are not okay to keep around you. These things remind you of a life that you are trying to move away from. Now I'm not saying that you should completely throw away your sexy undergarments. But if they remind you of a time that you don't want to revisit, or they make you want to put yourself on display once you put them on, then you need to get rid of them. Tuck them in the bottom drawer of your dresser, hidden under some other clothing. Remember your triggers. If you are a visual person such as myself, you don't want to entice the eye any more than the everyday eye already sees in normal life.

Some will resort to adult toys to help them in their journey. On this issue I have gone both ways. I cannot tell you what is wrong and what is right because I don't have that answer. The best thing I can say on this subject is to talk it over with God and consult your conscious. If you believe it is wrong to have them, then it is wrong for you to have them. If you believe in your heart that it is okay to have them, then you do what you need to do. But above all else, make sure that you are at peace with God with whatever you finally decide.

I have used toys in the past (in my thought process), to keep me from picking up the phone and making a visit to someone's house that I had no business in. I have also tossed them because it didn't really help or it just made me want the flesh more. Bottom line - it's a personal choice that rests with you and your soul and one that allows you to sleep at night. Consult God in the matter and let Him direct you on your path.

25: <u>Speak</u> Your Present and Future into Reality (Control Your Mind)

Your reality is what you make it to be. Someone once asked me if my life was of my choosing. My first response was "no" because I wasn't where I wanted to be in life. Then I thought about it and realized that it *was* of my choosing. It was because I spoke it into reality. Just as you speak good things into reality, you can speak bad things into reality. The thought begins in the mind and then moves to the lips and into the air where it becomes life and reality. Spoken words attract people, things and situations to you.

If you want to be successful in your celibacy walk, your walk with God and anything else that your heart desires, all you need to do is first think it, speak it and then live in it. Once in the air it *will* call to it all the energy it needs to become viable. "I am celibate. I am a servant of God. I am obedient to the Lord and His will for my life. I will wait for God to send my spouse to me. I am preserving this body that God has given me so that I may carry out His will for my life. I do not abuse this body that God has given to me because it and I belong to Him, so I am not misusing His property by intimately sharing it with someone who God has not designed for me as my spouse."

God being the merciful Father that He is knows that sometimes we will fall down and misuse this body that He has given to us to use. The key is to not stay there, but rather get back up and keep striving to do right by and for our Heavenly Father who loves us dear. I've leaned on Mary Mary's song *"If I Fall"* to help me through such times. The song is a very upbeat song that talks about not focusing on or bringing up your past failures, but to get back up, trust in God to help you and to keep it moving! This song has helped me many times when, while trying to do right, I find myself falling short. It's okay to fall down every once in a while (God knows we will), just don't stay there!

Even though God has everything under control, we must still do our part in this journey. We begin by taking control of our mind and controlling what comes out of our mouths. We must be guardians of our minds (the thoughts that we think) and of our mouths (the words that we speak). We must learn how to capture the thoughts and the words that go against our goal and convert them into thoughts and words that will successfully propel us through to the end of our journey. When we think and speak words of discouragement like, "I can't do this! It's too hard!" we must capture and convert them to thoughts and words of "I can do this! This is not too hard for God and me!" This is how we are able to be successful in our celibacy walk!

* * * * *

So now we have a good, strong and solid foundation to build our celibacy walk upon. Congratulations on your success thus far! If you haven't started doing so already, you may want to begin keeping a journal to record your experiences in this journey. During my walk there were times when I faced a challenge and overcame it. Then there were other times that that same challenge came about and I wasn't so successful. In the aftermath, I would rack my brain trying to figure out why I was successful in the past and not successful in the present. Had I been more diligent in my journal keeping, I could have turned back to those pages to find the answer and arm myself for the next adventure.

So where do we go from here now that we've laid the groundwork? We go on to the next sections that help us to deal with living a life of celibacy on a daily basis. In Section II we will talk about walking daily as a Single Female. In Section III we will address the daily walk of being a Single Male. Don't feel limited by your sex in regards to what section you read next. Although the sections are geared toward male and female individually, there is something for everyone to learn and use in each of these two sections.

After you complete Sections I through III, make sure you spend some time in Section IV, whether you're in a relationship or not. Although you may not be in a relationship at this very moment, you may one day be in one and you'll want to make sure that when that time comes that you are prepared. Say you wanted to go for a drive in a car; you didn't wait until that moment to learn how to drive did you? No. You learned prior to your desire, so when you were ready to go, you already knew how to do it. It's the same principle here. Prepare the way for that current or next relationship now, so that you can increase your chances of being a successful celibate couple!

If you're already in a relationship, read Section IV together and commit to being a celibate couple. Allow the *Covenant Pledge of Celibacy* to commit you two to celibacy in your relationship in the same way that a marriage certificate commits a married couple to monogamy in their relationship. Sign the pledge together and frame it just as a married couple does with their marriage certificate. This is just as important to the single celibate couple as the marriage certificate is to the married couple. Allow it to encourage and strengthen your commitment to God, to yourself and to each other in your successful walk of celibacy!

SECTION II

For the Single Woman

26: Don't Get <u>Caught Up</u> in Event or Holiday…Drama

Each season can bring with it several opportunities to present you with "drama" in one fashion or another. If you're not careful, they can lead you to seek out or accept invitations that are best left unanswered. For example, a friend's wedding, a new love entering into the life of a close friend (especially if you don't have one of your own), a high school reunion or any event where you're "expected" to have a date or significant other. But especially those events where you are highly likely to hear at least 10 times, "So when are you getting married?" These events and holidays are geared to send you flying into the arms of an old lover for comfort if you aren't careful.

One thing you can do when you're asked that dreaded question, "When are you getting married?" is to simply reply, "When God says the time is right." If they're single, turn the question on them and ask them the same. It does two things. First, it takes the focus off of you and gives you a little breathing room. You've instantly regained your confidence regarding whatever stage of life you're in and you no longer feel the need to run to a man for safety. Second, it makes people think twice about asking you such a question that puts unnecessary pressure on you in this area of your life. If you're single, there is a reason why. You could be working on yourself or your relationship with God. You could have some goal that you'd like to achieve prior to marriage; you're actively looking but just haven't found him yet (or shall I say, *he* hasn't found you yet); or you simply have no desire to get married. Whatever the reason, it's yours and you shouldn't have to justify it to anyone.

27: <u>Remember</u> What You "DO" Have, Not What You "DO NOT"

Women tend to be the more emotional of the two sexes; it's a widely accepted observation. Being emotional is simply a part of our makeup. It can be a good thing, and it can be a bad thing. It's all in the way that you look at it. Realizing this, we need to acknowledge that sometimes when women get lonely, we start to think about all the things that we don't have. This tends to make us feel sad and lonelier than before. So what do we do? We try to fill a gap that we think or feel is there by doing something, *or someone*, we shouldn't be doing. We begin to rationalize and convince ourselves the reasons why we should go and be with someone.

"I'm a good woman. I deserve to have someone. I'm attractive and I have needs. Besides, I'm only human." And the ever-popular, *"I'm not married, so I'm not hurting anyone."*

To all those reasons I say, "STOP!" Don't kid yourself! Take the reason, "you're not married and that you're not hurting anyone," for example. My response to that - Exactly! You are not married and therefore you *shouldn't* be sleeping with anyone. PERIOD! So how do you get past the lonely days? We'll talk about some practical steps to help with this as we continue on. The first step is to stop feeling sorry for your self. We jeopardize who we are and our self-respect when we wallow in self-pity.

The reasons listed above and the countless others we could come up with are all lies straight from the devil. We don't have to accept these lies because God provides for all of our needs.

The thief does not come except to steal, and to kill, and to destroy. I have come that they may have life, and that they may have it more abundantly.

–John 10:10

Another key factor to remember during these moments is that no man wants to be with a woman who doesn't have self-respect. And if he does, you need to run like he's holding a gun to your head because believe me, if you don't respect yourself then neither will he. It all starts with love and respect for God, and then for yourself. If you are going to be successful in your journey you need to be firmly rooted in love and respect for God, and then for yourself.

It is so important that you get this. This is why I said it twice, so listen to these words. If you have this foundation in place, it makes this step easier because instead of spending time focusing on self-pity, you are focusing on the blessings you have in your life, big and small. Whether it's your health, a job, freedom to come and go and do as you please, or whatever it is, embrace it! When you focus on your blessings you realize that gap that you thought was there is but the size of a pinprick. To help you do this, start a daily gratitude board. Each day when you awake write one thing that you are grateful for on it. It will be a constant reminder of how blessed you are!

Here's a critical point to ponder. If God had given you some of the things that you asked Him for years ago, would you still have those things today, or would you have lost them because you weren't yet ready for them? When I look at the woman I am now versus the woman I was say ten or even five years ago, I can honestly say that if God had brought my husband to me then, chances are great that I would now be divorced. I was in no way ready for that type of relationship during that time in my life, as I had believed myself to be.

If you don't have something when you think you should, thank God! It only means you are not, or were not, ready for it. Chances are you would have just messed it up, along with messing up some other people in the process. When God determines the time is right, He will bring it, whatever it is, to you. At that moment, you will recognize the truth in these words.

28: Bring a <u>Female Friend</u> to a Holiday or Special Occasion Event

Bringing a female friend, instead of a male friend, to an event will make it a lot easier to attend holiday or special occasion events because there is no chance of crossing the line from friend zone to something more. If you happen to cross that line, this book cannot help you. Turn the event into a girls' night out. Get dressed up and go have fun just hanging out with your friend. It'll be a lot easier than going alone or with a male friend who you may or may not have feelings for beyond friendship. Even if you haven't in the past, this is a time when those feelings can, and sometimes do, develop.

During these events you see all the couples there that seem to be enjoying each other. Now imagine what it would be like if you took a male friend. He's dressed up and smells better than you ever remembered him smelling before. He just got a new hair cut and he is wearing his suit like nobody's business! You know the one that show off all the work he's done in the gym. To top it all off, you've had a few drinks. He asks you to dance and your mind starts wondering "what if?"

Now you're in trouble. So what do you do? STOP! Rewind this whole scene in your head right up to the point where you start to ask him to attend the event with you, and then you STOP! Instead, go ask a girlfriend to accompany you, and avoid this whole scene all together.

29: Stay <u>Active</u> in Activities or Social Circles

One of the worst feelings we can experience is self-doubt or self-pity. During the holidays or seasons of special occasions when it seems as if everyone you know is enjoying positive changes in their lives like getting married or engaged, buying a new house, or moving to a new city, you suddenly find yourself in that mode of self-doubt. It's important that you not be alone at this time.

If you are in a mode of self-pity, it is much easier to fall deeper in. You're happy for those who are doing so well. But then you wonder when something good is going to happen to you. Next thing you know you're eating a ton of cookies and ice cream, drinking your cares away at a bar, or falling into the arms of an old lover. These situations are exactly where you don't want to be.

You can prevent yourself from falling into these situations, by working on a project or hobby that you've always wanted to do and didn't have the time previously to dedicate to it. If you have time to have self-pity, then you have time to do something constructive. Use this time to focus on something good and you will soon find that you are so enraptured in what you're doing that there's little time for much else, let alone self-pity.

You can also get active in your community and various social events through to the bigger events. Start by asking a friend to go with you to a networking event where you'll have an opportunity to meet other people. If someone is hosting a party or small get-together, ask if they need help with the planning or sending out invitations. It gives you a chance to know in advance who is coming and get the inside scoop on someone that might have similar interests as yourself. This can be a great start to a potential new friendship. (This works for both sexes, it doesn't have to be a future love interest, but it could be your new BFF!)

The point is to do something. If you're not, you're giving the devil an open doorway to come in and tempt you in areas where you don't need to be tempted. We've all heard the saying, "idle hands are the devil's playground." Let's make sure we close that door and rebuild our self-confidence in the process, especially when we see how much others are enjoying our company.

30: <u>Sow</u> into Someone Else's Life

There are multiple reasons why you would want to sow into the lives of others. Because it is the right thing to do, it makes you feel good; it pleases God and much more. So how does this help in the walk of celibacy? Well, I'll tell you. It distracts you from self, it keeps jealousy at bay and it strengthens your toolbox and helps you to recruit new soldiers into your army. Let me give you an example.

A friend of mine who I hadn't spoken to in awhile was getting married. She was going about her business, living life when it happened. Marriage, or even dating, was the furthest thing from her mind and then another friend suggested she meet her brother, thinking they might hit it off. My friend did meet her friend's brother (initially over the telephone, no doubt) and they talked for hours. During this conversation he decided that she was "the One," and thought they were destined to be married. She thought he was joking, but joking he was not! It happened because her friend thought to sow into her life. My friend has now been happily married for over ten years and has a beautiful little boy. She and her husband in this story were both walking the walk of celibacy and did so until their wedding night!

Hearing their story, I could have been jealous that she wasn't even looking when her husband found her. And maybe I was for a brief moment. But I decided that because this was my friend, that I was going to do all I could to help her be happy in this area. The way I did this was by helping with the preparations for her wedding.

Each Saturday we ran all over town from dress fittings to checking on the cake, to getting the broom for her and her husband to jump over. Whatever it was that she needed, I was there for her. It took my thoughts off myself and it strengthened our friendship. By my actions, I showed her that I cared for her and was truly happy for her. It also gave me courage in my walk and showed me that there are men out there willing to wait until the wedding night to be intimate with the woman they love. It gave me the resolve to help me accomplish six plus continuous years of celibacy!

Now I'm not saying that because you sow into someone else's life that God will bring you a husband. No. What I am saying is that because you chose to be a blessing to someone else, whether you knew it or not, God will in turn allow someone else to be a blessing in your life. Just think, all because someone thought to sow into my friend's life, my friend was blessed! Because I chose to be happy for my friend and support her in her wedding preparations, my strength in this walk was increased. You never know what blessings God has for you or for someone else when you sow into the life of others. By sowing into someone else's life, you remove jealousy from the equation and open the door to your future blessings.

31: **Spend Time Figuring Out <u>Who You Are</u> and What You Want**

What are some of the reasons that people have casual sex (for the purpose of this book, any sex outside of marriage is deemed casual sex)? The main reasons are hormones and sexual desire. If you started having sex in your teens or early 20s, chances are that peer pressure and the old adage that everyone is doing it had a lot to do with it as well. You wanted to know what it was like or didn't want to be left out. The guy you were dating convinced you that if you really loved him then you'd have sex with him. These reasons are attributed to the beginning of many sexual revolutions. If you don't know who you are and what you want, it's easy to get caught up in these excuses and begin or continue to have sex.

Once you're in it, it's hard getting out of it. On the other hand, if you start out with what you want in mind, it's a lot easier not to fall into the mode of having casual sex. I have a friend who is 35-years-old and is still a virgin. She's educated, intelligent and a nice looking woman who has dated and fallen in love before. Yet, she's still a virgin. The reason being is that she knew who she was at an early age and wanted. She knew that she didn't believe in casual sex. She knew that she wanted to wait for marriage. She knew that as a Christian it is her rightful and respectful service to God. This knowledge makes her celibacy walk a little bit easier.

Instead of thinking about reasons why you should have sex when the urge hits, think of reasons why you shouldn't. Add the things that you want (and want to accomplish) with your celibacy walk, to the reasons you shouldn't be having sex and now you're armed to complete another day, another week, another month and beyond in this journey.

32: **Get a Personal <u>Coach</u>**

One of the best gifts ever given to me was by a dear friend of mine. She gave me the gift of a personal coach. A personal coach is there to help you with whatever goals you need help with. You tell them what you want to accomplish and the kind of help that you need to support you in achieving this goal. Your goal can be professional, personal or anything that you are struggling to achieve on your own.

One of my goals was to create my own website called AYellowButterfly.com. It dealt with the issue of celibacy and helping others on their journey. Creating this website helped me to stay focused on my goal. By telling others what I was doing, I felt obligated to stay the course during the times that I thought that maybe I might not want to. By sharing this goal with my personal coach we were able to set weekly tasks and deadlines that I was held accountable for. Because I knew I had to answer to my coach for my actions or inactions, I was able to meet my goal of publishing my website which stayed up for several years and was visited by people all over the world.

In addition to helping you with your celibacy goal, your personal coach can help you with other areas of your life. But don't just take my word for it. Many successful people such as U.S. presidents, CEOs, Oprah Winfrey, Michael Jordan and many others have, or have had, personal coaches. In the cases of Oprah and Michael Jordan, we've all seen how working with a coach worked for them. I'm just saying!

33: Create a <u>Vision</u> Statement/Board

One of the tools my personal coach armed me with was a vision board. This concept is also talked about in Rhonda Byrne's best-selling self-help book *The Secret*. It's not only helpful in your celibacy walk, but your life overall. The purpose of the vision board is for you to sit down and think about what you want to accomplish in your life and then put it on paper (or a big poster board). The purpose for writing it down is to keep it in front of you for inspiration, motivation and putting it into the world so it can return to you (calling it into action – we'll talk more about this later). Several of the items on my vision board were buying a house, creating my celibacy website AYellowButterfly.com and creating this celibacy book. As of today I can tell you that I have accomplished all of those things and am well on my way to accomplishing the other items on the board.

So exactly what do you put on your vision board? Put any major goal that you want to accomplish. It can be something big like starting a new career, buying your dream car, becoming a better friend or something as small as losing weight and keeping it off. It can be in pen, crayon, marker, pictures, or however you want it to be. Items can cover half the board or a tiny corner. If you want to be successful in your celibacy walk, put it on the vision board so you know that it's a goal that you're working toward!

34: Keep Your <u>Goals</u> Posted before You

So you've spent time figuring out who you are and want you want. You got or thought about getting a personal coach and you've created a vision board of the goals you wanted to achieve with your goal of celibacy being part of those goals. So what do you do now? You post your goals and keep them in front of you at all times. You live, eat, breathe and sleep these goals. You do this so you know what you're working toward. You do this so that you can track your progress as you go along. You do this so you can celebrate the goals you've achieved, or partially achieved. You also do this to help you set your next set of goals.

In many people's homes, you'll see something that is important to them cradled in a frame and posted on a wall for all to see. It can be a college degree, professional certificate, portrait or photos of family and friends or a favorite piece of artwork. You frame them because you are proud of them. You enjoy looking at them and they motivate you or just simply bring you joy. The same thing goes for your vision board. You want it to motivate you. You want to celebrate the things on it you've completed and you want to show it off to others.

But it doesn't stop there. Write your goals out on a sheet of paper or on your computer. Print it and make multiple copies and post them everywhere. Place it on your bathroom mirror, your refrigerator, inside of the door leading to the garage or the inside front door of your house, your steering wheel, your checkbook or wallet. Post it anywhere that you can and will see it on a daily basis. In addition to posting your goals, set deadlines for your goals where applicable. This is another method to keep you moving forward. I used this technique when I was writing my first screenplay. I taped it to my bathroom mirror so I would be facing myself when I looked at my goal and thought about my progress, or lack thereof.

Each week I set a page goal for how far I needed to be in the script. I gave myself enough time to allow for life to happen and still meet my goal. If I was a little behind by the end of the week, I knew I had to make some adjustments in other areas of my life to stay on task. Setting a time line to my goals helped me to reach them and complete my screenplay. It's easy to become lax in keeping your goal or to stay celibate if you're at a moment of weakness and you're not constantly being reminded of what you are working toward. Make it hard for yourself to forget your intent by keeping it forever in front of your eyes by posting it all around you.

35: Improve on One Aspect of You/Your Life

Achieving a personal goal in one area of your life gives you more confidence and experience in achieving future goals in your life. Take exercise for example. If you're not used to exercising, starting can be a little difficult at first. So you start with taking a walk around the block. After a few days your body begins to build up strength in your legs and before long you begin to get used to the extra exertion and now you can walk up to a mile or more in no time. After three weeks of walking you've now developed the habit of walking and you're looking to add to your workout regime. Now you decide to take on yoga. You always wanted to but didn't think you had the flexibility. Because you're now walking, you have increased flexibility and now have more energy to take on yoga with more ease and enjoyment today than you could have a month prior.

Now let's apply this to the celibacy walk. Let's say you chose exercise as the one area that you wanted to work on in your life. You've already shown yourself and others that you are capable of reaching your goal by the new, leaner and fitter you. Your overall persona and mood has improved. You are more confident. You feel wonderful inside and outside and you want to expand this good feeling to other areas of your life. When you were sexually active, it felt good or even great during the time of the encounter. But how did you feel when it was over?

If you were on the celibacy walk and you slipped up, you probably felt bad because of the choice that you made that went against your goal. When you're feeling good about what you're doing, you don't want to do something that could and will possibly make you feel bad about yourself. If you slip up with your celibacy, it seems that it would be easier to slip up with your exercise, because you've already slipped up with celibacy, right? Wrong! Because you already have one success under your belt, it's easier to pick yourself up, dust yourself off and get back on track with reaching your goal.

Remember, this is a journey that is taken one step at a time. If you're halfway on the road to your destination and the end point is in your sights, how much sense would it make to just stop and turn the other direction? Absolutely none! Make sure to arm yourself with successes in other areas of your life to help arm you for success with your celibacy walk.

36: <u>Define</u> Your Limitations

Defining your limitations is not about making excuses for failure in your walk. Not at all! It's about determining what you can and cannot subject yourself to during this walk. If having two or more drinks suddenly puts you in the mood and you start dialing numbers of past lovers (been there), then maybe you want to limit your beverages to one or even non-alcoholic drinks until you have some time and practice at being celibate under your belt. If being in attendance at certain social situations causes you to feel lonelier than other events, you might want to steer clear of them until they bother you less or not at all.

I have a friend who will not go to concerts (musical, comedy, or otherwise) if he's not in a relationship because he doesn't want to subject himself to seeing couples enjoying themselves together when he's alone. Initially I thought that was a little extreme. But as I gave it some thought I understood where he was coming from. He recognized that although the event was something that he enjoyed, doing it alone was going to put him in an uncomfortable position. So instead, he chose to honor his comfort needs. He defined his limitations and operates accordingly.

Being celibate doesn't mean that you have to stop living or doing the things that you enjoy. It means you have to learn what your weaknesses and triggers are and adjust your daily tasks in those areas until you're stronger and more equipped to deal with them safely. Defining your limitations early on will help prevent you from walking into a situation that could have easily been prevented had this been done from the start.

37: <u>Be Realistic</u> with Yourself

Defining your limitations is critical in the journey that you've embarked upon. It is equally important that you are also realistic with who you are, your limitations and what you realistically can and cannot handle. In Section I, I talked about a soldier in my army who was also at one point the love of my life. I had successfully rung up six years of celibacy and I believed that I had this thing licked and that I could have him over to my new apartment and be totally fine. I mean, after all, we were very close friends and he knew me better than almost anyone else. I still loved him, and in some respect always will. But at the time of his visit, I didn't think I was still *in* love with him.

WRONG ANSWER! I was still in love with him and it was not a very good idea to be alone with him in my home. I was unrealistic about my feelings for him, and unrealistic about the control I thought I had over my emotions. I don't need to tell you what happened. We didn't go completely all the way, but it wasn't for a lack of trying! We went as far as my body would allow us to. This was a man who had been my lover and who knew what I liked and took great care to please me and make sure that I was completely satisfied and wanted for nothing after an evening with him. Even at the sake of his own full gratitude, he released it to my fulfillment. This was one of the things that I treasured so much about him; that he loved me beyond himself.

And again I say, I thought I could handle him being in my apartment, alone, with me. I was doomed from the moment he rang the doorbell! I was not realistic with myself. So instead of reaching a true eight years of unbroken celibacy, as I like to believe myself achieving, I actually achieved six and two. I know as women we all have men or events that we say, "don't really count," but let's be realistic here. If your foot breaks the threshold, it counts! Had I been realistic with myself about my true feelings for this man that I still loved at that time, I wouldn't have had an asterisk toward the end of my eight years.

38: Create a Daily/Weekly Journal

If you want to get your finances in order or lose weight, the very first thing an adviser or counselor will tell you to do is to keep a journal. You're asked to do this so you can see where your money went or what you ate that day and how it impacted your bottom line in a good or bad way. If you have a little extra money at the day's or week's end, or lost a couple of pounds, you can go back and look at your journal and see how you accomplished that goal. The reverse is also true. You can see where that donut or sweet potato you ate added two more pounds than you previously had before consuming them.

The same principle works for your celibacy walk. The things you want to capture in your journal are the things that gave you strength in your walk and the things that caused you to stumble or even fall. If you slipped up and got off track (as it may happen, especially when you first start out), make sure to detail what happened, how you got there, what you were feeling before, during and afterward. The afterward is very critical to include because you can use this to remind yourself of the hurt that you felt when and/or if you get to the brink again and are teetering the fence. Being reminded of those bad feelings can be enough motivation to prevent you from going there again.

Journaling is also useful in helping you to release your guilt from mistakes that you've made. It can be valuable as a part of the healing process. It can show you things that can be triggers for you that you had no idea were indeed triggers. It will give you insight to your emotions and behaviors in a way that simply relying on memory can't provide you with. It is also your written testimony to share with others who are on the same path. You don't have to share your most intimate thoughts with others, but utilize it to help refresh the experiences in your mind. Pick and choose what you do wish to share.

Actions are also critical in this walk. Recording the actions that prevented you from going through with an encounter is also a part of your toolbox (see Section I for more info on creating your toolbox). There were times when I ended up somewhere I had no business being because I didn't stock my toolbox well in the beginning. Following that event I would rack my brain trying to figure out how I was able to escape that fate the last time my craving became that strong. Sometimes I remembered and other times I did not.

When I starting tracking my thoughts, actions and events in my journal, I was able to catch myself in the midst of going down the wrong track. I'd pull it out and see what I did successfully the last time I was feeling that way. I was able to repeat that step, action or whatever it was and once again be successful with my celibacy intact! You can also use entries in your journey to help you encourage someone else that is on the walk when they are teetering and need support. Remember, we said it before -- iron sharpens iron!

39: Stock Up Your <u>Library</u>

The celibacy walk is more than just abstaining from sex outside of marriage as we've already talked about a bit earlier in this book. We've talked about it being a spiritual, mental and emotional walk, in addition to the physical realm. We are a whole being made of bits and pieces, so we must address each of these pieces as they all work together for the good of the whole. That said, the contents of your library should not only be about where you've been and where you are, but also where you want to go.

If you want to be a married woman, you should be preparing yourself for that stage in your life, using this time of singlehood that God has granted you with. Think about the kind of wife you want to be and do some self-evaluation to see how close or how far you are from there and then begin building your library in that area. If marriage is not in your future, think about and figure out what *is* in your future or what you'd like your future to be and look for books in that area. Use this time to build yourself up in whatever area you've determined, either through self or guided evaluation, could use work. Then use that as your starting point for stocking up your library.

To help you get started or to enhance your current library I've provided some titles that you may find helpful. Of course we all know the greatest and most important book in your library is your Bible. There are also many other books and resources that are helpful as you travel along the path. We mentioned a few of the items in Section I that can be helpful to you in stocking your library. There are even some books that will help you with your celibacy walk (see below for a list of a few that I have found). Some of these I own, some I've read and some I've only skimmed. Take a look and use this partial list as a starting point to building your library.

Improving on the Love Walk:

- *The Five Love Languages for Singles* by Gary Chapman
- *The Five Love Languages of God: How to Feel and Reflect Divine Love* by Gary Chapman
- *The Purpose Driven® Life* by Rick Warren
- *Lord, Teach Me How To Love* by Dr. Creflo Dollar Jr.

Those Seeking Marriage in the Future:

- *Before We Say I Do: 7 Steps to a Healthy Marriage* by Rev. Marvin A. McMickle
- *Created to Be His Help Meet: Discover How God Can Make Your Marriage Glorious* by Debi Pearl
- *Love & Respect: The Love She Most Desires; The Respect He Desperately Needs* by Emerson Eggerichs
- *The Excellent Wife: A Biblical Perspective* by Martha Peace
- *A Wife After God's Own Heart: 12 Things That Really Matter in Your Marriage* by Elizabeth George

Walking in Celibacy:

- *The Power of Abstinence* by Kristine Napier
- *Abstinence - The New Sexual Revolution* by Marilyn Morris
- *Celibacy Equals=Life: About the Ultimate Personal Relationship* by Carla Bagnerise
- *Celebrating Celibacy* by Kathern A. Thomas
- *Freeing Celibacy* by Donald B. Cozzens
- *Celibacy: A Way of Loving, Living, and Serving* by A.W. Richard Sipe
- *Celebrating Celibacy* by F.S. Mitchell
- *Sensual Celibacy: The Sexy Woman's Guide to Using Abstinence for Recharging Your Spirit, Discovering Your Passions, Achieving Greater Intimacy in Your Next Relationship* by Donna Marie Williams**

** I have not read this one yet but the title was so interesting that I couldn't pass up including it!

40: <u>Call</u> Your Life into Action

Now faith is the substance of things hoped for, the evidence of things not seen.

–Hebrew 11:1

So Jesus answered and said to them, "Have faith in God. For assuredly, I say to you, whoever says to this mountain, 'Be removed and be cast into the sea,' and does not doubt in his heart, but believes that those things he says will be done, he will have whatever he says. Therefore I say to you, whatever things you ask when you pray, believe that you receive them, and you will have them."

–Mark 11:22-24

The common theme and denominator of both of these scriptures is **Faith** and the calling/belief in things that presently appear not. One of the rages of 2006 was the self-help book and movie *The Secret*. Below is an excerpt taken directly from their website http://thesecret.tv/living.html:

"The Secret teaches us that we create our lives, with every thought every minute of every day. Living The Secret offers tools and ideas to help you live The Secret and create the life of your dreams."

Any way you put it; the bottom line is the same. You have to speak it and believe in whatever it is that you wish to accomplish in your life. If you believe it, *really believe it*, and live it, align it with God's word, walk in it (daily), it will come to pass. It may take some time, but it will happen. The key things to remember are to align it with God's word (in the Bible), pray on it, believe in it, walk in it, and allow God to bring it to pass in HIS TIME. Not on your time, but in His time. He has already told us in the Bible that His word will not come back void.

So shall my word be that goeth forth from My mouth; it shall not return unto Me void, but it shall accomplish which I please, and it shall prosper in the thing for which I sent it.

–Isaiah 55:11

While you're on your celibacy walk you have to call your success in this area into existence. It's simply vocalizing everything that we're talking about here in this book. Vocalize it and give it life. Give it breath and wings to fly and to call those things that are needed, unto you, to help you in achieving your goal of celibacy until marriage. By speaking it aloud, you will also be calling out to the man who is willing to walk this path of celibacy right along side you.

I experienced a real life example of calling life into action. I was born and raised in Cleveland, Ohio. I always knew that I would one day leave, that Cleveland was not my home. I had a few job opportunities to leave but they weren't right for me or didn't work out. The first was with a good company and with people I believed I would have enjoyed working with. But the job was in a small town in Michigan and I knew I wouldn't like the city and in time, I would begin to dislike the job, seeing as it was my only reason for being there. A second opportunity was in a city with a Fortune 100 company. With the tragic events of 9/11, which took place within the same time frame, my on-site interview was pushed back a month. During that time, I interviewed and had been offered a job with a bank in Cleveland that was willing to pay for my master's degree in English, so I stayed.

About four years later I had moved on to another bank that was bought out less than a year after I started and I was informed that my department would be laid off. I saw this as my opportunity to finally leave Cleveland for good. The lease on my apartment and my last day at work were both in the same month, and I decided that I was moving to either Arizona or Nevada. I put all my things in storage and temporarily moved in with my parents because I had no intention of renting another place in Cleveland. I was out of there. Every time someone asked me what I was going to do or where I was going to go, I said I was moving to Arizona or Nevada. They asked if I had a job or leads on one. I told them no, but that I was going before the winter came (the previous winter was the worst winter on record and I had had enough and refused to do it anymore).

I filed for unemployment and had to attend a workshop on job searching. I attended and told the instructor there was no need for me to be there because I was moving to Arizona or Nevada and was not even looking for jobs in Cleveland. She too asked if I had any leads in those states, and again my answer was no. She asked if I was sure that I didn't need their help finding a job there and I told her no! She saw my steadfast determination and wished me luck and sent me on my way. Shortly thereafter, something in my spirit told me to pack up the few things in my parents' house because I would be soon leaving. I did what I was told and kept looking for jobs out of state and started getting my car ready for the road trip.

Then one day something told me to go apply for a job at a particular company. I thought 'I'll do it in a minute.' But my spirit said 'move now.' So I did and applied for two jobs. Within two to three days I received a call for both jobs and was scheduled for phone interviews. The following week the company flew me out to Phoenix for a face-to-face interview (this was the same company that wanted to fly me out just prior to 9/11 that I mentioned earlier). A few weeks after my face-to-face, I was in my new apartment in Phoenix, Arizona!

It is possible to call your future into existence. I am living proof. I am still calling my husband and children into existence and know that when God is ready to bring him, He will. First I needed to complete this book and begin my life as a full-time freelance writer. Oh, and I called that (full-time freelance writer) into existence too, along with leaving Phoenix. At the time of publishing, I am now a full-time writer living in Gallatin, Tennessee. Call your life into existence; it works!

41: <u>Speak</u> to God Daily – Build Your Relationship

This should be an easy one, something that we should be doing everyday. For most of us just about every minute of our day is planned out due to the numerous obligations that we have from family, friends, jobs and anything else that requires our time. For some, this is more than enough on their plate and trying to fit anything or anyone else onto it is just asking too much. We don't want to think that we put God on our "to-do" list or even on the back burner, but some do it every single day. How many times have you said, "I'd spend more time reading my Bible if I had more time in the day" or "I'm just too tired to pray tonight?"

We've all been there. A lot of times I wait until the end of the day, after I've done everything else I need to do and just before going to sleep to pull out my Bible and try to read, when I know that my mind is half past dead. As Christians, this is just not going to do it. If it takes us scheduling time to spend alone with God on a daily basis, then that's what we need to do. There are many opportunities that we have every single day where we can spend time with God. It could be in the shower, in the car or while cooking dinner. Any time that you aren't actively engaged in conversation or interacting with someone else, is an opportunity to spend time with God. Spending time with God can occur while you're listening to a gospel CD, taking in a flower blooming or observing a sunny day. It doesn't have to be some elaborate, sketched out event or encounter.

Simply enjoying the creations of God is just one way to connect with and build your relationship with God. When you acknowledge God in your daily tasks, you open up yourself to increasing and building your relationship with Him.

As you walk through this journey of celibacy, the most important relationship you will need to carry you through is a strong relationship with God. If you currently have a good relationship with God, that's excellent, continue to build on it. If you'd like a much stronger connection and relationship with God, but are not quite sure where to start, use the suggestions mentioned previously.

Begin talking to God on a daily basis (even if it's just while you're walking to the bathroom or break room at work). It will increase your desire to learn more about Him and engage with Him more. You will start to look to Him for guidance and assistance in every area of your life. This in turn will drive you to learn more about Him, to seek Him through His word (the Holy Bible) and your prayer life will increase. The thing to remember about prayer is that it is a conversation with God. Many people have conversations in their head all the time, thinking about what to cook for dinner, preparing a list for your trip to the grocery store, et cetera. Having a conversation with God is the same. The only difference is that He will speak back to you. You only need to listen.

There are times when a prayer closet is essential, but there are also times when you just need to speak to God right then and there, right where you are! You just need to begin the conversation. If you don't know what to say, tell Him that and He will meet you right where you are, wherever that is because He loves you that much. When you know that you are loved, you want to return that love. You return it in actions, thoughts, words and whatever it takes to express your love. One of the ways that we can reciprocate God's love for us is through our celibacy walk. Another way is through building on our relationship with Him. It's as simple as having daily communications with Him.

42: <u>Join/Start</u> a Singles Ministry

The beauty of a singles ministry is that you have a built-in support system with other Christians who very well may be on the same journey you are on. Because you are in a church setting, the topic of sex is not going to be readily discussed as in a non-church setting, especially if their sessions are held at the church, which most are. But that's okay, because you will not always be at the church. This is an opportunity to help you build on some of the other things we've already talked about here in this section and in Section I. (*indicates items found in Section I)

- ***7: Fill Your Toolbox** – This is a great place to find a Christian mentor or prayer partner. It is essential as you walk this road, to have someone to call upon to help strengthen you and offer guidance.

- ***8: Gather Your Army** – Having friends and family in your army is wonderful. But sometimes you need someone who knows exactly what you're going through because they too may be going through a similar situation. This is an excellent place to find someone that is highly likely to be on the same path as yourself.

- ***23: Surround Yourself with Like Minds** – Everyone's experience with this celibacy walk is going to be a bit different simply because we are all individuals. Those who are alike in mind and journey may catch you from going off the path much sooner, than someone who is not on the path would catch you. Those traveling the same path can usually see it sooner than those who are not. Remember iron sharpens iron!

- *29: Stay Active in Activities or Social Circles* – Many singles ministries have social events and activities that you can partake in.

- *41: Speak to God Daily – Build Your Relationship* – Every instance you spend with God, either in a group setting or alone, is an opportunity to build on your relationship with God.

Many mid- to large-sized churches will typically have a singles ministry. If the church you attend doesn't have one, check with someone who attends another church and see if they do. If neither exists, then talk to your pastor about creating one in the church. If you are interested in having one, I guarantee you there are other singles in the church who are in want of a singles ministry as well, and some of those people may be willing to help you start one.

All you have to do is to get started and more singles will begin to join. It only takes one person with the courage to get it started and many will benefit from it! Another option is to join or create a Singles Ministry MeetUp® or Celibate Singles MeetUp® group. A benefit of a MeetUp® is that it is not held in a church and may be more enticing to non-Christians who want to be part of such a group but prefer not to be associated with a church. An added benefit is that as you work in the singles ministry, you will find that your relationship with God will greatly improve. He will provide you with the guidance and support that you need. He will draw others to you and to the ministry and it will be a great success!

43: Form a Sister Circle

A sister circle is simply a group of good girlfriends that you can call at any time of the day or night to help you in any area of your life. These are women who know, support and love you regardless. *Regardless!* Now, not everyone in your sister circle will be your best friend, nor is every woman supposed to be.

Think of your sister circle as your wardrobe. There are some women who you grew up with or have known for years. They know you better than anyone else, sometimes including yourself (think of this friend as your favorite pair of jeans). There are women you've only known for a few years but feel like you've known a lifetime (a comfy new plush robe). There's the friend who you can always count on to lift your spirits and is always up for having fun and a great laugh (your go-to party dress or outfit). Then there's the woman who is like a fine tailored suit, the smart woman who is the voice of reason who cares enough to call you on it when you're not being your best. And we can't forget about your fiercest pair of high heel shoes that are super comfortable and can go with any outfit from casual to chic to glamorous! This friend may not always be there when you *want* them, but they are always right there just when you *need* them, just like God!

Individually, these women are phenomenal in their own right, but together they become a stunning wardrobe to the stars! One of the things I used to do with my sister circle was to have a monthly Lady's Night Out/In. Each month we'd get together and either have dinner out at a restaurant, or over at someone's house. When it was a night in, we'd have themes ranging from just desserts and wine nights, to chocolate nights or potlucks. We'd celebrate birthdays (complete with tiaras for the birthday gal), births, a new promotion, or just being fabulous women!

The only rules with the sister circle were that all the women had to compliment and encourage each other because we were there to uplift and support each other. Sister circles can be a great enhancement to any woman's life. Your circle can be as big or as small as you'd like it to be as they are there to support you and for you to support them. Just be sure to follow the rules (supportive and encouraging women) and have fun!

44: <u>Encourage</u> Yourself to Go beyond Your Everyday Norm

We've talked several times about celibacy being more than just physical, but mental, emotional and spiritual as well. On the journey you will begin to find out new and exciting things about yourself that you never knew; things like courage, strength, determination, tolerance and ingenuity, to name a few. You already know of many of the qualities that you currently possess, but you never know just how much a quality actually resides within you until it is tested. You will find that you have courage at levels that you didn't know were present within you.

You don't have to go around touting your courage and announcing your celibacy by wearing a wristband (like the ones I created for sale on my website when I first started this) if you choose not to. But you will want to share your experiences with others to help encourage them, as well as yourself. As you begin to speak about your experiences with others while on your journey, you will begin to see your courage grow and blossom brighter than you ever could have imagined. The added benefit that's true about encouraging others is that you may start out with the intent of helping others and find that the words that you speak, from the heart to others, can and many times will be encouraging to yourself in a way that you may not have known you needed.

Strength and determination will also present themselves to you to as you ride along the road of successful celibacy. These are traits and tools you will need to cultivate, nurture and increase while walking the walk to keep you going each day. There are many things that others can do to help you on this path and they will all be necessary. But you also need to be able to stand before the mirror and talk to the person staring back at you. You need to learn how to drive yourself and to build up your own thickness of skin. You can read all four sections of this book, get helpful tips, encouragement and guidance to help you on this path, but you're also going to need to dig deep and come up with ingenious ways to specifically help *you* be successful.

There will be days when you simply want to give up and quit. But that's when you need to dig even deeper. That's when you come face-to-face, directly with the real you. When I was in basic training in the Army Reserve, I went through most of the training not being able to do a push-up. When I was in formation and the whole platoon was doing physical training I could get away with not really being able to do the push-ups because no one was paying that close attention to me.

One morning, I wasn't paying attention and was called out of formation to do push-ups in front of everyone. Luckily some of the other girls had been working with me prior to that morning, lifting weights and helping me to improve on my form to build up my muscles. Because I had other soldiers supporting and encouraging me, I believed I was much stronger and maybe I was capable of completing a set of ten push-ups.

When I got down on the ground to actually do the push-ups, I had to really dig deep and believe in myself that I could in fact do them. It was the courage, strength and determination that I had built up inside of me that I would complete all ten, that allowed me to be able to actually do ten correct push-ups! I was so proud of myself when I completed them and stood up. By the time I left training, I was up to over 30 push-ups! I was able to reach this feat because I pushed myself when I didn't think I could.

From that moment on, I adopted a mentality that there was nothing that I could not do. I began to take this mentality with me throughout the rest of my life and it has served me in many ways. I believed in myself enough to keep going many times when I was scared and thought that I couldn't make it. I remembered the courage, the strength and the determination that I gained in basic training and I use it even today to fuel me to keep pressing on to accomplish whatever goal I need to in life.

I can pass along the things I've learned through my walk and tell you all that God has given me to share with you, but the rest is up to you. The rest has to come from within. As you do this, you will begin to see yourself in a new and exciting light. You can take the wonders that you've learned about yourself through this walk and begin to apply it to other areas of your life. Take what you learn about yourself traveling through the world of celibacy and allow it to propel your everyday life to the next level. If you can make it through this walk, there's nothing that you can't make it through!

As you take each step in this celibacy marathon, you will learn something new about yourself. You will harness new skills and tools. You will progress in areas that you previously didn't think you were capable of, or to the level that you are now achieving. And you will sharpen life skills that will propel you and make you successful in every area in your life. I've said it before and I'll keep saying it, your celibacy walk isn't just about sex and your abstaining from it. It is but a means to show you who you are, enhance your inherent traits and draw you closer to and allow you to be a better servant to God.

45: Spend Time <u>Loving</u> You

There are many reasons that we have sex outside of marriage. We have a sexual desire that we believe we need to fill. It's part of the relationship that you're in. You have a need to feel desired and wanted by a man. You're trying to fill a void. For some, it's a matter of boredom and/or simply something to do. But ask yourself this question.

In the midst of having sex outside of marriage, how true are you being to yourself and your feelings? By this I mean, if you are a Christian and strive to walk and live a Christian life, how does it make you feel to know that your actions of non-marital sex are counterproductive to your Christian walk? How do these acts impact your overall self-worth and image? How much do you truly love yourself if you're engaging in a practice that is going directly against your core beliefs and the God that you love and so desire to please?

These are questions that I found myself asking every time I stepped outside of my celibacy walk. I wondered how much could I really love God if I kept making the same mistake over and over again? I knew even before I entered the bedroom of the man I loved that when it was all said and done, I would feel miserable and question my commitment to God. We both knew that following our lovemaking; I'd be so upset that he would need to comfort me. This alone should have been enough to make me not put either of us through this again. But it wasn't enough to make me stop. Days later when I reflected back on what I had done and the thoughts I had prior to going over to his house, I had to ask myself some of those same questions that I posed here. I had to dig deep within myself to find the answers. When I was being real with myself in answering these questions, I came up with one central theme and that was that I did not love myself to the best of my ability. There was usually some area of my life where I wasn't happy and at that time I used sex to pacify myself. If I wasn't feeling loved by family or friends, I'd turn to having sex with a man that I knew loved me and that I loved. If I wasn't happy with my job or my self-image, a roll in the hay would always make me feel better, or so I thought.

Now this is not to say that I only had sex with him when I was feeling bad about myself and needed a pick me up, because it wasn't. I loved him very much and he was my first love. So many of the times that we were together was because I loved him and it was but one of our ways of expression. In the beginning, like many people, I didn't really see much of an issue with pre-marital sex. I mean I knew what the Bible said about it but I chose to do what I wanted to do because I was more concerned with pleasing myself than following the words of the Bible.

Luckily, God's love for me wouldn't allow me to continue on the path that I was on. It seemed that more often than not, my pastor's sermons had something to do with being true to one's self, loving God and obeying His commandments and abstaining from pre-marital sex. There were Sundays where he would pointedly say to the congregation that if we were not married then we had no business being in bed with anyone, period! It seemed that the sermons were coming at me at every turn and they would not let up. Sometimes I swear that my pastor was looking and speaking directly to me. It finally got to the point where I had no other choice but to listen because it was not going away. My spirit had become convicted and I had to make a change whether I liked it or not.

This is how I first began my celibacy walk. After accepting the call to walk in and speak about celibacy to others, I tried to do it in my own strength. I tried to just stop where I was and move in a new direction. Now this was a good thing, a great thing actually. However, one of the things I neglected to do was to work on the inner me. In the process of changing my life and changing my behavior, I forgot to spend time embracing and loving myself, and everything about me. I thought I was good in this area. I mean I loved me and was good with me. But when I began my celibacy walk and began being tempted all the time, I became aware of areas within me that weren't as polished as I had once thought they were. These were items that the devil used to help weaken my resolve to be celibate and opened me wide open to falling back into old and bad behaviors. Had I done the work of spending time loving and strengthening me in every area imaginable, it would have been a much harder doorway for the devil to enter into to tempt me.

Think of it as a hurricane warning from the National Weather Service. You are warned that the storm is coming and that you must prepare for it so that there is minimal damage to you and to your property. You're instructed to board up your windows, make sure you have flashlights, a battery operated radio, plenty of batteries and a supply of food and water. When the storm comes you want to make sure to stay away from windows and get in a safe place, if you have a cellar or basement this is best.

If you've taken these precautions you will be well prepared when the storm hits.

If you only did *some* of these steps, but forgot to board up your windows, you've just exposed your windows to being broken in the storm. The same holds true with spending time loving *you* during this walk. If you neglect building your self-esteem or another pertinent part of what makes up *you*, when temptation arises it will now have an open doorway in which to enter through.

46: Keep Men Out of <u>Your Home</u> at All Times

Seems simple enough, but it must be said. Regardless of how strong you are or how much will power you think you possess, you are not as strong as you think you are when it comes to the walk of celibacy. As a celibate person you have to guard yourself constantly. You have to limit temptation wherever possible. This includes your home. I can honestly tell you that for years men outside of my family never entered my house beyond the front doorway. In the beginning I thought I was strong enough to allow a man to enter my house because I had been celibate for about six years. I was strong. I had will power and a resolve as strong as steel.

Then the one-time love of my life came over to see my new place. Remember, I told you earlier that this man was one of my most devout soldiers in my army who helped me on my journey. He left the next morning. I had to start over again with my celibacy walk. That was the last time that I let a man into my house. I don't care how much you think you can handle the temptation or how long you've been on the road to celibacy, don't fool yourself into thinking that you can handle being in the lion's den for long without being sniffed or bitten. Case in point, Las Vegas act Siegfried and Roy worked with tigers for many years and became so relaxed with the animals that when the lions were cubs Roy slept and bonded with them until they reached the age of one.

The trainers trusted and believed that they knew the animals and were certain that they could control them. They became quite comfortable and in turn, more lax with the animals than they probably should have been. Although the tigers were raised in captivity, they were still wild tigers by nature. The tiger's killing instinct never decreased or dissipated, it merely sat dormant until the tiger's nature overcame its training and it attacked its trainer Roy, almost taking his life. Siegfried and Roy had performed about 30,000 shows over many years with a multitude of large and vicious animals without any serious injuries, until that last time.

Some would say these guys knew what they were doing; they had it locked up tight. There was no need to worry because they had the animals under their control. But just as the tigers still have their innate killing instinct within, we as humans still possess sexual desires within ourselves. Given the right set of circumstances, and the slightest relenting of focus on your goal, you too can end up in a bad situation. If you keep men out of your house at **all** times, you will improve your odds of being successful in your celibacy walk!

47: Go to <u>Sleep</u>

This has to be one of the simplest and easiest things you can do to help you be successful in your celibacy walk, bar none! So I know you're asking how going to sleep will help you be successfully celibate. It can and it will. It's a three-step process. When you're experiencing an urge to have sex and feel like you're losing the battle and are destined to give in, the first thing you need to do is to stop whatever you're doing. Just stop. If you're picking up the phone, dialing a number, getting dressed for an encounter or anything else that you may normally do just prior to setting up this encounter, stop! STOP! Say a quick prayer and then go to sleep. When you awake the urge will be either gone or lessened to a manageable level.

The first time I experienced the power of sleep was by accident. I was in one of my moods, raring to go in the wrong direction. I went to pick up the phone to call my love. I started experiencing this internal struggle between knowing what was right and seeming to have no control of the hormones raging in my body. I started dialing the numbers one by one, very slowly trying to convince myself not to dial another number and to just hang up the phone. I did hang up, but I picked it up again and started redialing. It seemed liked I couldn't stop pressing those numbers. In a moment of sheer and complete desperation I said a quick prayer and asked God to keep me from doing what we both knew I was about to do.

Instantly, my eyelids became so heavy that I could barely keep them open long enough to hang up the phone. The next thing I knew I was in a deep trance-like sleep. I don't remember how long I slept; maybe it was an hour or so. But when I woke up, the urge was nearly gone and I had successfully made it through that temptation. When I was in that position again and my flesh was weak, I did the same thing each time. I stopped, said a quick prayer and I went to sleep.

When I realized the power of sleep as a tool in helping me to be successfully celibate, I began to tell others about it. And yeah, some believed me, and others laughed at me. I even told the man that I would usually call when I chose to give in, and he too laughed. Years later when he decided to take his own walk of celibacy he remembered what I told him about going to sleep and he tried it. He called me to tell me how well it worked. He admitted that he didn't believe me when I first told him about it, but desperate to stay committed to his goal he tried it and was amazed at the results. This was a man with a very healthy sex drive, but even he could not deny that it works!

So I'm sure you have a few questions like 'how can I go to sleep if my hormones are in overdrive,' or 'will I dream about sex while asleep,' or 'exactly how does this sleep thing work in curbing my urges?' I don't have all the answers, but I can tell you that there were times when I did dream about sex when I fell asleep and there were times that I didn't. But when I woke up, regardless of whether I dreamt about sex or not, I was still in a better state of mind when I awoke. In terms of actually falling asleep, it was only difficult to do if I didn't pray before I lay down to sleep. As to why it works, I'm not really sure why it does. It just does!

The key thing to remember is that in order to be successful using this tactic, you need to: 1.) Stop whatever you're doing; 2.) Say a prayer; 3.) Go to sleep. It's as simple as that, 1, 2, 3! Just keep in mind that in order for sleep to work in your celibacy walk, you must first say a prayer. It doesn't have to be long or drawn out, but it must be heartfelt and sincere. When you ask God for help, He will step in and help you. And you will have success!

When I tried to use sleep and didn't pray, I usually failed in my mission and ended up in his bed. When those times happened I looked back later to see why I wasn't successful that time, but had been at other times. The thing I found was that I hadn't prayed. When I hadn't prayed, it was also much harder to go to sleep. Pray, sleep and be celibate. Don't pray, sleep and start over again.

48: Increase Your <u>Prayer</u> Life

As you take your walk of celibacy you want to make sure that your prayer life is intact. And then increase it. During the beginning of my walk I think I prayed more then, than I had previously in my life. I was in my early 20s, had a very healthy sexual appetite and was in love with a man that I believed I would never stop loving. At that age you're in your sexual prime with hormones raging. You may be experiencing a whole new world of freedom. You're now living on your own. You are feeling your adult and womanhood, so you should be able to do what you want, or so you feel.

Your body desires to be pleased through sexual intercourse. You're old enough and grown enough to do it. You're thinking you should be able to do what you want to do. Plus, you've tried it enough to really enjoy it and you have a good understanding of how your body works and responds to pleasure. Plus everyone else is doing it! These are some of the things that you may be thinking at this age which makes taking on celibacy that much harder. This is why prayer is so important. If you pray now, you will need to pray even harder to help curb the emotions and hormones that are in overdrive during this time in your life.

You're in your early to mid or late 30s (where I am now), and most of your friends have husbands and kids. You've been on your own for years. You know who you are (or at least have a good idea). You're doing well in just about every area of your life but you're still single. Or you've been "good" (done all of the right things, however you define it), and you still don't feel like you are where you should be. You had a life plan and you've worked it and have done all the steps. Yet you're still not where you were supposed to be according to the plan and it doesn't look like there is any improvement ahead on the horizon. You start to wonder if it'll ever happen. You question if your living is in vain and wonder the purpose of continuing on this "good girl" path, if things are not where you think they should be and change is hiding from you.

Thoughts of this nature are the devil trying to convince you that God does not hear your prayers or that He won't help you in the areas that you've been praying for. Believe me, it's all lies straight from hell. Your prayer life is what is going to help you combat these thoughts. It is what will help you from giving in to desires of the flesh.

There may be times when you need to remove yourself from everyone and every thing and just spend time in prayer with God asking Him to strengthen you in the area of celibacy. Whether it's a prayer closet or putting your face flat to the ground and praying your heart out, you need to find that place where you can go and be one with God. He will meet us at the point of our need, we just need to turn to Him and ask Him for his help and we do this through prayer.

49: Don't Go by How Things <u>Look</u> or <u>Feel</u>

One of the hardest struggles with this walk of celibacy and in any area of life is to not focus on purely what the eye can see or what the heart feels. This is something that God still continues to remind me of on a regular basis. Let me give you an example of what I mean. For my 21st birthday I took myself to Vegas. While there I was walking down the strip viewing the sights and just enjoying my time there. During this stroll, something said to me, "You're going to be alone for a while." I thought, "Cool, I could use some me time to get me together." I was happy with this revelation, for a while at least.

Some 14 years later, I am still alone. Or am I? If I go by how things look and how things currently feel I would not be a happy person right about now. From the look and the feel of my current station in life, my journey of celibacy doesn't seem to be coming to an end any time soon. As I move further into this world of singlehood with the writing of this book and other ventures within this arena, it looks as if my hopes and desires of becoming a wife and mother are just that, hopes and dreams. If I go by how things feel, I might buy into that notion. But what I was told was that I would be alone for *a while*, not *forever*! The difference between those two words is great and important to note. If I hang my sights and feelings on the word "awhile," then I know that what I see and feel in the now, won't always be in my future.

As you're walking down this path of celibacy there will be times that you feel like taking this journey on is just too much or too hard to continue. But that is just a temporary position. Sometimes it may feel like you will explode if you don't have sex soon and that at any moment you're going to slip up. Remember that this is only a momentary feeling. You will have some bad days on this journey where you will feel like you can't take another step. You can't base the entirety of what you're doing on one feeling or what presently stands before you. You have to take that moment for what it is, a moment. Then you have to dig in and keep pushing; keep fighting for what you've already started. Don't give up on God, and don't give up on yourself.

Think about when a mother gives birth to her child. While she is in labor and pushing that child out her body, she feels like that child will never come out. She feels like she will live with that agonizing pain forever, that there is no end in sight. But what does she do? She bears down, grits her teeth and pushes with every fiber of her being. She keeps pushing and pushing until finally that baby comes out and is placed in her arms. When she first sees and feels her child in her arms, all that she experienced just moments prior, has disappeared and she is filled with joy. She knows that everything, all the hurt and pain were worth it for her to reach this beautiful prize she now holds in her arms. She has done it. She stuck it out and now reaps the reward. It's the same thing with the walk of celibacy. Remember, celibacy is not forever. It may look like it is, it may feel like it is, but it is not.

The walk will certainly sometimes camouflage itself as never-ending. Should you get married, you've reached your goal and you may now reap the rewards of sex, within the sanctity of marriage. However, should you never marry, (and I can tell you from experience) your sexual desire can, and will, have a way of whittling itself to a barely noticeable part of your conscience. If you choose to diligently be celibate for God and honor His commandment of not having sex outside of marriage, or even if you never get married, I guarantee He will provide your sexual desires a way out of the storm while honoring your promise and commitment to Him.

You are not alone on this journey. When things begin to play tricks with your eyes and pull on your heartstrings, know that God knows the plans that He has for you, for us all, and that they are designed to help you and see you through.

For I know the thoughts and plans that I have for you, says the Lord, thoughts and plans for welfare and peace and not for evil, to give you hope in your final outcome.

–Jeremiah 29:11 (AMP)

We also have to remember that our thoughts are not His thoughts. He sees what's ahead in our future, especially when we don't.

For My thoughts are not your thoughts, nor are your ways My ways," says the Lord. "For as the heavens are higher than the earth, so are My ways higher than your ways, And My thoughts than your thoughts.

–Isaiah 55:8-9

50: <u>Celebrate</u> Your Successes

Every day that you are celibate is a success, so celebrate it! Maintaining celibacy in a world that encourages you to do otherwise is a great feat and one that needs to be acknowledged. You celebrate when you achieve a milestone in many other areas of life such as when you've been on a job for a number of years or when you complete a degree, or anything else of importance to you. Apply that same sense of excitement to your celibacy walk. Celebrate what you and God have achieved together. Mark the date that you begin your journey on a calendar and celebrate it after you've successfully achieved celibacy for a month, six months, a year or more. You set the goal of when you celebrate and to what level your celebration takes on. Your celebration can be a trip to the spa, dinner with friends or purchasing something small that has meaning to you. It can even be a certificate of successful achievement that you can make on your computer. Print it, frame it and put on your desk or wall. Whatever it is, make sure to capture the milestone in some way that you can post it to look back on. Remember how you feel on this day, at this time. You will need to draw on this experience during those times when things aren't as easy as they are when you are celebrating your successful celibacy milestone. Following the celebration set a new goal and plan the next celebration all the way up to the ultimate goal of successfully achieving celibacy.

SECTION III

For the Single Man

Some of the things you'll find in this section may seem a little bit off the beaten path with respect to celibacy. But I guarantee you that they are all designed to help you walk this walk a little bit easier. Since men and women operate and think in entirely different ways, the approach to celibacy needs to be presented to each sex in different ways. You'll find this section to be shorter than the other sections in this book. That's by design. I hope to keep your attention by presenting the information with greater brevity. By doing so, it is my sincere hope that you complete this section in its entirety as many of the topics build on the previous topics.

The ways outlined in this section are designed to help you address sex beyond just a physical standpoint. They are geared toward addressing the heart and the soul of man, as well as the physical side of man. It's designed to connect you to your core being and to show you how these things and your sexual self are interrelated and interdependent. Men are by nature providers, protectors and purposeful in their behavior. This section is written in such a way to address these areas of man and to establish and strengthen the connection of these traits to the practice of celibacy.

51: Build on <u>Your Relationship</u> with God

The most important relationship you'll ever have in your life is the relationship you have with God. At different points in your life your relationship will shift, based on your needs and where you are in your life walk. Traveling down the road of celibacy will be one of those life-altering events that will change and reshape your relationship with God. The relationship you have with God prior to, during and following your celibacy walk will differ. You will learn new ways of seeking and communing with God during this time, as He will be your lifeline.

We all think we are strong enough in and of ourselves, for the most part, to handle whatever comes our way. Men are strong and are designed to be the head of the family and of the household. It is thought, by some, that men should be able to handle whatever comes their way. And this may be true, but not alone. Think back to the days that Jesus walked the earth and performed many miracles. If we look at these stories through the natural eye, we would conclude that Jesus relied solely on Himself, without seeking the Father for assistance. But if we look through our spiritual eye, we will see that even Jesus looked to His father, God, for aid in achieving the goals that He was tasked with.

And He said, "Abba, Father, all things are possible for You, Take this cup away from Me; nevertheless, not what I will, but what You will."

–Mark 14:36

A man once told me something to the effect of whatever he needed, it was up to him to accomplish; that if he couldn't do it himself, then it couldn't be done because he was the only one he could truly rely on. I don't need to tell you that this is archaic and irrational thinking. What it says is that this man has a flawed relationship with God. If Jesus looked to God for help, who are *you* not to do the same. Regardless of the depth of your relationship with God, it is critical that you turn to Him through every step of this journey. You cannot do it alone. Build your trust in Him even stronger, and you will be better for it!

52: Read and Learn What <u>The Word</u> Says about Pre-Marital Sex

Just about everyone knows someone else who has spouted statements such as, "If God wants me to stop (fill in the blank), then He needs to personally tell me so!" If you can't recall anyone saying this to you, chances are that it was you who spoke these words. Guess what? He already did! If you doubt that He has, then pick up any Bible in any translation and read it for yourself.

On the subject of sex outside the sanctity of marriage, the Bible uses the terms *fornication* and *sexual immorality*. So that there is no confusion, we will define these terms. Merriam Webster (used for all definitions) defines *fornication* as, "consensual sexual intercourse between two persons not married to each other." *Immorality* is defined as, "the quality or state of being immoral." For the purposes of this book we will use Webster's first definition of *marriage*, "the state of being united to a person of the opposite sex as husband or wife in a consensual and contractual relationship recognized by law." This means a legal ceremony performed by someone who is authorized to do so.

It does not mean someone you've been living with (common law marriage) defined as, "the cohabitation of a couple even when it does not constitute a legal marriage," or someone you've had a child with or have been dating for an extended period of time. So now that we are clear on the terms *fornication, immorality* and *marriage*, let's look at what the Bible has to say on the subject.

...Now the body is not for sexual immorality but for the Lord, and the Lord the body. ...Do you not know that your bodies are members of Christ? Shall I then take the members of Christ and make them members of a harlot? Certainly not!

–1 Corinthians 6:13, 15

For this is the will of God, your sanctification: that you should abstain from sexual immorality.

–1 Thessalonians 4:3

Beloved, I beg you as sojourners and pilgrim, abstain from fleshy lusts which wars against the soul.

–1 Peter 2:11

But fornication and all uncleanness and covetousness, let it not even be named among you, as is fitting for saints.

–Ephesians 5:3

Marriage is honorable among all, and the bed undefiled; but fornicators and adulterers God will judge.

–Hebrews 13:4

Now you can no longer plead ignorance of God's word on the subject of sex outside of marriage. If you were seeking an engraved invitation or formal letter from God telling you not to have sex with anyone other than your wife, you have it written out and repeated numerous times. God has done this so that there is no mistaking His stance on this subject. You've heard the saying, "when you know better, you do better." You have been informed, there are no longer any excuses!

53: Spend <u>Time</u> Praying and Fasting

Earlier in this section we talked about building on your relationship with God. There are many ways that you can do that. The main ways people utilize to spend time with God is through the reading of His word (the Bible), time spent in prayer and attending church from Sunday morning services to weekday Bible study. These are all great ways to commune with God, but we also have the gift of fasting. If you're not familiar with fasting or the benefits of it, you may be curious to know how "starving yourself" can improve your relationship with God, or help you in your celibacy walk. When I first heard of the practice, I too wondered the same. But trust me, it can.

Fasting does a few things: it serves as a sacrifice to God. It gets His attention; it focuses your prayers; it opens you up to better hear from Him; and it cleanses your body internally as well as a number of other benefits. Fasting also helps you distinguish His voice from other voices that may enter into your mind. Remember, the devil is also able to place thoughts in your head. When you fast, you learn to hear God's voice and what it sounds like so that you are not confused when you hear it again. When you hear a voice that is not His, you can capture it right away and strike it down with authority in the name of Jesus.

Fasting is not just about not eating. There are a number of different fasts that you can try. Some fasts, such as the Daniel Fast, requires that you consume no beverage other than water and that you only eat unprocessed fruits and vegetables. There are also fasts where you cut out certain foods such as sweets, or where you might consume nothing from sun up to sun down. There are a variety of fasts that you can find on the Internet to help you in this process. You can follow them to the letter or you can alter them. Ultimately the choice is up to you, as is the length of time that you fast.

The thing that you need to remember is to have a purpose in mind for your fast. If you are struggling in your walk and just not getting enough help from any source that you turn to, try fasting to gain strength and courage in your walk. Whether your purpose is to seek guidance from God or just to show your love for Him through self-sacrifice, it is important to have a goal that you can hold on to when your body begins to react to the lack of food it is receiving. As you fast, spend the time that you would normally spend eating, in prayer. Tell God what it is that you are seeking, then listen and wait for Him to respond. Your answer may not come immediately during or following the fast, but keep listening and you will surely hear from Him.

54: Respect Your <u>Spirit</u>/Honor Your <u>Body</u>

So often our spirit speaks to us and so often we don't listen. Let's say you're planning an evening out and something inside you says that maybe you should stay in tonight. But you've made plans, you paid in advance, you're dressed and you're ready to go, so you do. Somewhere during the evening an event occurs where people are hurt, including you. Not badly, but enough so it's a nuisance that you certainly could have done without because it is going to cost you time and money to rectify the situation. As you're sitting there in the aftermath, something says to you, "I told you, you should have stayed home!" That voice is your spirit talking to you. Now you're thinking, "I should have listened, then I wouldn't be in this mess."

Your spirit is there to protect you and to prevent you from harm, so listen to it. In John 16:6, Jesus speaks of sending a comforter to be with us. The comforter is God who resides within us in spirit form. We know that God is alive. We know that Jesus is alive. Yet we cannot see God or Jesus in the physical form. We feel God and we feel Jesus in our spirit and therefore know that He is real. By having respect for the authority of your spirit and the God that lives within you, you allow your built-in support system to aid you through difficult times.

The walk of celibacy will be one of those difficult times, but your spirit will help you. When your spirit tells you that you have no business calling that woman or going to her house, listen! It is there to help you maintain your celibacy. When you commune with God on a continual and never-ending basis, when you respect your spirit, you make this walk of celibacy a little bit easier. It only has to be as hard as you make it.

When you learn to regularly respect your spirit, respecting your body becomes second nature and that much easier. We want to make sure that we respect our bodies because they are not ours alone. They belong to God. In case you were wondering exactly what the Bible says on the subject of respecting one's body, see the following.

Flee sexual immorality. Every sin that a man does is outside the body, but he who commits sexual immorality sins against his own body. Or do you not know that your body is the temple of the Holy Spirit who is in you, whom you have from God, and you are not your own?

–1 Corinthians 6:18-19

55: Get a Male Role Model/Mentor
Organizations such as Big Brothers Big Sisters, corporate mentorship

programs, trainers, personal advisors/coaches, internships and the like, all exist because we in and of ourselves do not have all the answers that we need to be successful in every area of our lives. In high school and college, each student is assigned academic advisors whose job it is to guide, direct, listen and support every student through their educational process. When you start a new job, chances are you will be shadowing someone who has been at the company for some length of time and that is experienced in the job or the department that you are now working in. In all of these instances, you welcome them and are grateful for their aid and assistance.

The same applies in your celibacy walk. This book is a great guide and offers advice in your walk. But you can't tell this book about a challenge that you are having and get a personalized response that is geared toward your immediate situation. You can get that support and encouragement from a role model or a mentor, especially one that is or has walked the path that you are currently walking.

Michael Jordan and Tiger Woods are arguably the greatest athletes of their respective sports. They have God-given talent that no one but God can take away. It is theirs; they own it and they have forever shaped the way that their sport is played. Yet, even they have had mentors and/or roles models that traveled the path before them. They looked to those people to help them figure out where they may have gone wrong with a play or for a way to improve upon a play in a future game or tournament. They could have said that they were already great so why seek the help of others. Tiger and Michael didn't because they knew that there was always room for improvement. A mentor or role model committed to your success will offer you this same level of support and leadership.

56: Have a <u>Reason</u> to be Celibate

Most men operate in purpose and therefore, must have a reason for why they do the things that they do. If something has no value for that man, watch and see how long that man will continue to perform that action or devote his time to it. When the value of an entity diminishes for a man, he reduces his time with it and eventually moves on. This is most readily and easily seen with men who constantly date multiple women. As soon as that woman has met that man's needs in whatever area he's lacking, she will begin to receive less attention, fewer texts and finally no response to her calls to him. When value disappears, so do a man and his actions toward that subject.

Take any area of importance to a man and ask him why he does what he does in that area and that man will have an answer. If he doesn't, chances are that area is no longer a part of his life.

Why do you go to work each day?

"To provide a life for myself and possibly a family in the future."

Why do you work out on a regular basis?

"To relieve stress, to be healthy and to look good."

Why are you celibate?

???

Make sure that you have an answer to the question of why you're celibate that holds significant enough meaning and value to you personally. If you don't have a meaningful answer, how likely are you to continue in this walk of celibacy if you haven't established a rock solid purpose and goal for your walk? If you can think of no other reason, let your reason be because you desire to please God in this area and because He has commanded in His word for you to be so.

57: Keep Your Mind <u>Right</u>

Once you have your purpose for instituting this practice and goal of celibacy into your life, make sure that it becomes second nature to you. Recite it in your head. Recite it aloud over and over again so that when you are asked about your journey you have an answer. You should be able to speak your purpose without hesitation or doubt and with true conviction. You never know when you will be called upon by God (or others familiar with your journey) to encourage someone else who is considering taking the vow of celibacy, or who may be struggling with a challenge in staying true to the course. If you falter, your integrity in this area may come into question.

In addition to being a beacon to others, you will also need to encourage yourself when you're having a bad day and just want to go back to your old ways of having sex outside of marriage. If there is nothing to convict your spirit of backsliding, your hormones may convince you that you have done enough and that there is no longer a need to continue on this journey. You may begin to think that what you've done is good enough. It is not. This is a lie straight from hell. You haven't done enough in the way of celibacy until you have exchanged wedding vows before an authorized official and you have been pronounced "husband and wife."

58: Set <u>Standards/Limitations</u> for Yourself

So you've developed your reasons for being celibate that are now a part of your heart, your soul and your core being. You've worked to fully wrap your mind around everything concerning your celibacy walk; all of you are in agreement. So what's next? Now you must protect the work you've just done. Time to call ADT®, Brinks®, buy security cameras, multiple locks and call in the armed guards to protect your celibacy. Sounds like I'm going a bit overboard here? Not at all. You will need all these measures and more to guard your celibacy.

I don't know if you know this or not, but war has just been declared upon you.

The moment that you made it up in your mind to be celibate and locked this goal into your DNA, the enemy was placed on alert with orders to be ready to strike at an instant notice. Women that you have always wanted but who previously wouldn't give you the time of day, because they only saw you as a friend or were always in a relationship when you weren't, will suddenly have you on their mind. You will now become their mission. They will now openly welcome you into their arms and into their beds. You will run into them at the grocery store, the gym and even at church. They will be in the best shape in their life and eager to show you.

Previously these women were shy in their approach or conservative in their dress. That shyness has disappeared and their skirts are a little shorter than you remembered. Their cleavage has seemed to increase in size as they have gained weight in all the right places and lost it in all of the bad places. But not all the women who approach you will be of this variety, some will be the good girl next door. These women will come in many shapes and forms. So be on guard.

This is what we call war. In war you need to establish your boundaries, and determine what exposure you will allow these women to have to you and in what context. These women have absolutely no place being alone with you in your home. Late night conversations about what she's doing or what she's wearing are off limits. Phone sex is totally and completely outside the universe because it has the power to give you the impression that you're okay. This is harmful thinking. Because in fact, you've just opened your top-secret security files and exposed them to the enemy. They know your weak spots and you are ripe for a major attack. Make sure that your guards are always on duty and that you're always ready to fight the good fight. At some point, you will have to fight. It's up to you to make sure you win.

59: <u>Evaluate</u> Your Relationships with Women

Begin to evaluate the women who remain within your camp. If you are in a relationship with a woman, ask yourself why this woman is here? Is this a woman who can support you in your celibacy walk? Is she a woman who is willing to take the walk with you? If the answer is yes, she can support you, and if she is willing to walk with you, then you need to ask yourself what place does this woman have in your life, short and long term? Can you can see her in your future and in what capacity is she in?

If you can see this woman as a potential mate and mother to your children, then this is a relationship you need to work on in other areas outside of sex. Learn whom she really is, what makes her tick. Learn how she communicates and expresses herself outside of the bedroom. If you don't see this woman as a potential mate and mother to your children, then it's time to move on. Gather your wits about you and let her know that the time has come for you two to part and go your separate ways. When you do this, make sure you deliver the message respectfully and in love. You don't have to be in love with someone to speak to them with love. Just because she is not meant to go the distance with you, doesn't mean she isn't meant to go the distance with another man. Make sure you leave her in excellent condition for the right man.

60: Let Your Mind and Spirit Dictate Your Journey

If you thought your hormones and sex drive had a mind of their own before beginning the walk of celibacy, you are in for a surprise. At times, your hormones will go into overdrive and it will be more tempting to just give in and let them have their way. But remember, up to this point you have put in a lot of effort to maintain your celibacy. Use the tactics you've learned in this section as well as those in Section I to help guide you to success.

Let your mind and your spirit be your conscious. Rely on your relationship with God to strengthen your resolve to stay committed. Rely on the support of friends, role models and your desire to please God. Don't give your hormones or your emotions more power than they deserve. Although emotions can be a mighty force, the mind can be immensely superior.

There is a reason why it has been said that a war can be lost in the mind before a foot ever steps on the battlefield. What occurs in the mind, can and will dictate what happens in reality. When your hormones and emotions try to convince you that you've lost and you may as well go and enjoy yourself, remember that your mind has the power to effect and change the outcome in your favor of succeeding in your walk of celibacy.

61: Get Your House in <u>Order</u>

There was a time when it was the norm to see two parent homes where the father was the head of the household. In most of these homes the mother stayed home and cared for the children and the home. With the existence of wars and men being pulled out of the homes, mothers were required to go to work to support the family and to keep the plants afloat. Given the opportunity, women developed an appetite for earning their own funds and excelling in a job outside the home. Somewhere along the way with all this massive change occurring, things became eschewed. Women became more independent and men began to feel less needed, and the roles that fathers once held became less of the norm.

With all this shifting in the homes, the order became lost or greatly diminished and damaged. But there is no need for this to remain that way. Somewhere along the way some men (not all men) lost the courage and fortitude to maintain and restore order in their relationship and subsequently, in their homes. So what do I mean by restoring the order? No, I don't mean that we need to go back to women in the homes and men being the sole providers. In today's society, there is a need for both sexes in the workforce. What I mean by restoring the order is to first start with you, the man. Restore the mentality that men are the providers, the head of our homes. This doesn't mean sole providers and we're not talking only in terms of finances. There was a time where men directed the family spiritually, emotionally, physically (just by virtue of being present and active in the home), and in many other ways, as directed in the Bible.

And men here's a secret, many women today desire you to be the head of the household. We don't desire to emasculate you! We just want you to take your rightful place in the relationship and in the home. Because many men have relinquished (again, not all men) their roles, women have had to step in and take the reins. Some women have held these reins so long that they don't know how to release them, even if they desire to do so. Women just need to know that men are willing, ready and able to take the lead again. We're not asking for anything more than what is already inside of you. So what does all of this have to do with celibacy? Everything! Men start by restoring women's faith that you have put, and will keep, your house in order. When you walk down this road of celibacy you instantly let the women in your life know that you have regained the reins and that you are on the path to being the man of your house and of your future family. If you are currently with a woman and you make and implement this decision, it lets her know that you are serious about order in your life and in your home.

If the woman agrees and goes on the journey with you, you are that much closer to completing your journey of celibacy because you are probably with the right woman. If she doesn't agree with you, then you know my motto: Keep it movin', but give it to her right. As you put your house in order, you draw yourself closer to the right woman and to success. If you are one of those men not meant to marry, you establish yourself as a model to encourage other men to bring order to their houses and to begin this walk right along with you.

62: Spend Time in a <u>Woman</u>'s Shelter

Now this is probably not something that you thought you'd find in a book about celibacy, but go with me here for a second. Up to this point we've talked about respecting your spirit, keeping your mind focused, setting standards and evaluating the women in your life. For women sex is emotional. For men it is physical. These steps are all geared to help you think of sex in more mental, emotional and spiritual terms.

If sex is just an act to you, it is easier to give in to the urges and impulses of your hormones. But if sex becomes spiritual and emotional to you, then your approach to engaging in it will be different. This is what we've been working on up until now. Now let's take it a step further and look at women from another perspective than you have in the past. Most men view women from a sexual perspective. If it's a woman they care about, they see and appreciate other facets of her outside of her body. Outside of the women in your family and a few other important women in your life, how often do you see a woman outside of the eyes of sex, either positively or negatively? Chances are not often.

So how do you reshape that? Well, one way to do that is by viewing women in different circumstances. As an example, try volunteering in a women's shelter. This can give you a first hand opportunity to see another side of women. You have a chance to learn the things that some women have gone through at the hands of other men. When you can connect with a woman on an emotional and/or spiritual level, you can begin to see them as more than just sex. When you can see a woman as more than just sex, you can see the importance of preserving her born again virtue (celibacy), and in turn, preserving your own virtue. When you can value and appreciate the benefits of celibacy in your life and begin to see women, as more than sex, the protector in you will also want to see and support celibacy in women. Thus, making walking the journey of celibacy a little bit easier. I challenge you to volunteer in a women's shelter and see how it changes your life.

63: <u>Respect</u> Her Like She's Your Mother/Daughter

Although spending time in a woman's shelter is an excellent way for you to gain another perspective of women, not all men will do so. I know this. But there are other ways to increase your level of respect for women. It is still important for you as a man walking in celibacy to see and understand women beyond that of a sexual being. Now on first reading, this may weird you out a bit, but again, go with me here and you'll begin to see how this works and how it can help you in your celibacy walk.

The next time you see a woman in your surroundings and your hormones begin to line up and begin the march to entice you to think of her in a manner other than platonic, close your eyes and picture this woman as your mother or your daughter. Then remove yourself from the equation and see yourself as some random guy mentally planning to approach this woman who is your mother or your daughter. How does it feel seeing that man approach her with the goal of nothing more than getting into her pants and tossing her aside when he's done?

Now open your eyes and see yourself looking at that same woman with the same level of respect as if she *were* your daughter or mother. See this woman that you are about to approach. How strong is that desire now to be with her sexually? Chances are not that great. How much easier is it to squelch those primal urges and maintain your celibacy in the face of these circumstances? For many of you, it will probably be a lot easier now that you can see her as more than just flesh.

A man told me the story of the courtship of he and his wife. They met, dated for a few months, and then began having sex. The sex lasted about three or four months. The day following the last time they had sex (he still remembers the date of the last time), he told her they needed to talk. What he told her was that they needed to take sex off the table. He told me that he knew that as long as they were having sex, he would just see her as another woman that he would soon tire of and move on. But he saw something in this woman, something past sex. She too agreed that they needed to wait. For the next ten months they continued on in their relationship without having sexual intercourse.

Their vow of celibacy continued until the night of their wedding. What this man learned by abstaining from sex was how to love and appreciate that woman in other ways that had absolutely nothing to do with her sexual body. As of the time of this book being completed, they have been married five years and are expecting their first child. This man learned to respect that woman as if she were his daughter or his mother. Subsequently, she became the "mother" to his "daughter!"

64: Think about the <u>Consequences</u> before Acting

One can find many positive things to say about sex and provide you with many reasons for engaging in the act without the benefit of marriage. But as there are two sides to a coin, there is also the adverse aspect of having sex outside of marriage. The standard responses would be disease and unplanned pregnancies. These are not desirable consequences for many people but they do exist. Imagine meeting a drop dead gorgeous woman who has all the physical and tangible assets that you desire in a woman (intellect, financial ability and stability, likes sports, great cook, etc.), and she is just as into you as you are into her. You meet and go out a few times. After a few dates you go back to your place and spend a few hours together having fun. When it's over, she doesn't require you to hold her and even gives you your space by going home. You think you've got it made. A few days later you're preparing for work and you're relieving yourself. All of a sudden it feels like someone just set off a bomb in your urethra! You are burning and blood is trickling down from your body in an area that blood should not be exiting.

Another scenario is that you're out with your boys having a few drinks and you start flirting with a woman at the bar because she's buying drinks hand over fist. You drink a little more and now a woman you wouldn't cross the street to meet is becoming more attractive and your boys start singing Ludacris' "*One More Drink.*" Next, you find yourself spending the night with this woman. The following morning as you begin to sober up, you become disgusted with your behavior from the night before. You rush her out the door and thank God that it's over. Nine months later you get a call saying you're going to be a dad and the paternity test confirms it, now you're stuck!

Now it doesn't have to be that dramatic. You could be a man who doesn't even drink or hang with the fellas that often. Your hormones could just be getting the better of you and you're tired of being celibate. You could wind up with a woman that you think is cool, but in no way are you interested in her beyond what's in between her legs. She's interested in you so you go for it, thinking everything is everything. The relationship is casual and she may even be seeing other men. Things are great until one day she ends up pregnant; you're worried until you remember that you always used protection with her. But then there was that one time when it broke. She tells you not to worry; it isn't yours. You start to think that if you had maintained your celibacy, you could have avoided all of this and you get back on the path. A year later you get hit with child support papers and a request for DNA, which of course matches. This is a story that actually happened to a man I knew who was walking in celibacy and decided to lay off his walk for one night. And guess what, like you'd be in the scenario I just described, he was stuck!

These scenarios won't apply to all, but maybe to a few. Unfortunately, these aren't the only consequences to having sex outside of marriage. You've grown closer to God and have built a strong relationship with Him where you trust Him for all your needs and you're enjoying life more, living in obedience. But even still, your body is telling you that you need to satisfy it and you just don't think you can take another night of not being with a woman.

You decide that you're just going to have to do what you've got to do and you'll ask for God's forgiveness afterward. So you call up an old faithful who has just been waiting for you to come to your senses. You sleep with this woman who is not your wife. As you're in the act, your spirit is telling you that you shouldn't be there. It's not as good as it was in the past, which shocks you because it was *always* good with this woman. Your spirit and heart are spent because you betrayed God and your vow; and your body isn't even satisfied.

Say you meet this great woman who instantly, at first sight, you know is the One. She is also practicing celibacy and asks you if you do as well because she sees you reading the paperback version of this book in a coffee shop while you're trying to get back on track. Now you have to look her in the eye and tell her that you've lost your way and have to start all over again. But you don't want to tell her this because you don't want to see the disappointment in her eyes. You don't want her to think that you're not a strong man. If you tell her the truth, you may see disappointment, but then again, you may not. You don't want to take that chance.

But if you don't tell her, you just lied to her and you've started your relationship off on the wrong foot. These are just a few of the consequences that one does not think about, but should when making plans to stray. Think and deliberate on them when you feel like you just have to give in, and then turn back to this book for steps to help you stay on the path.

65: Have the No Sex <u>Discussion</u>

There was a time and age when women expected men to be the head of the household. Guess what, we still do! There is nothing more appealing and comforting (to most women) than a man who can, and will, take the lead of the family, and before the family, the relationship. Now this doesn't mean that women want to be told what to do or that we don't want our opinions to not be requested and considered, because we do.

What it does mean is that we desire the man to take the lead in initiating decisions and discussions. We know that if the man initiates the conversation of celibacy that he is all in; we can trust that he will carry through with walking in celibacy. We know that this is a man that we can trust with our hearts and our lives. He has shown us that he respects and honors his own, as well our body by removing sex from the table. It also tells us how important God is in his life and that he has high moral standards, ones that we want to live with and pass on to our future children. It tells us that this man is a keeper because he has set himself apart from the rest of the world and has a strong mind of his own.

But there is one thing to note here that can be a negative, yet positive side effect of opening the celibacy conversation. Some women will see this and then be turned on enough to want to sleep with you that much more because you've shown her that you respect her soul, mind and body. The good thing about such an occurrence is that this kind of woman has just identified herself as one who is probably not meant to walk this journey with you, as she doesn't fully grasp the concept of celibacy as outlined in the Bible and in this book. Therefore, she should be cut loose because she can and probably will convince you to give in to the other side of celibacy. You don't need an Eve (a temptress), when what you're striving for is a Mary (a virtuous woman)!

66: Be a <u>Mentor</u> to a Young Man

Celibacy is not just for adults, as our teens are having sex as well. Their reasons have much to do with not knowing how to handle their hormones and the never-ending deluge of peer pressure. In order to help curb teen pregnancy, disease, and emotional issues related to having sex too soon, we need to set our youth on the right

path early on and address the issue of celibacy with them as soon as possible.

We can provide them with literature, such as the teen version of this book and Hill Harper's "Letters to a Young Brother." But the most powerful resource available to help our teens in this area is the example of a man walking in celibacy. Think how much good we can do in the youth population by reducing the number of teens having sex outside of marriage. By being the role model you also draw these young men closer to God and help to lay a much stronger foundation in preparing these young men for our young women who will one day be the heads and leaders of families and society. You're teaching these young guys how to respect women and how to ultimately treat them in a manner befitting to a young woman.

Being a mentor to our youth is a critical necessity. There are many men who can tell you their stories of how their lives were changed and shaped for the better by experiencing mentorship in their lives. Sometimes all a person needs is to be able to talk through their feelings and encounters with someone they can respect. Someone that has, or is going through a similar situation can help them to achieve success.

The added bonus in being a mentor to a young man is that now you have additional reasons to be celibate. First, you have someone looking up to and respecting you. Second, if you break your vow of celibacy, you may temporarily alter your self-respect (in this area of your life), and won't be able to look your mentee in the eye. But because you love and appreciate the respect that you have gained from your mentee, and you know how breaking your vow will impact the young man you're mentoring, you now have greater motivation and reason to not give in to your desires. The mentor and mentee relationship is beneficial to you both in the walk of celibacy and one that should not be overlooked or taken lightly.

67: <u>Stay Out</u> of the Strip Clubs/Compromising Places

Not every man will be one who goes to strip clubs. Most men, at some point in their life, will end up in a place that can stimulate their hormones to such a high level that will make them consider compromising their goal of remaining celibate. For some men that place is the strip club. For other men, it could be a place like Hooters or even a lingerie store. If you're a man who loves to look at and see women in lingerie, then it's probably not a good idea to go undergarment shopping with a woman. When you're in the mall, you definitely want to keep walking when you come across a Victoria's Secret or Frederick's of Hollywood store.

Keep in mind, compromising places aren't just public places, they are any place that will allow you to relax your guard to the point where your celibacy walk is in jeopardy. The most common place is your most comfortable place, the home (either hers or yours). Limit the amount of time that you spend alone with a woman in her home. Many people like to rent movies and stay in for the evening and just relax. You can still do this, but limit the kinds of movies that you watch. Limit the hours that you're watching the movies and the physical distance between you two while watching movies.

Try to choose movies that are comical in nature or ones that don't require or tempt you to want to snuggle because it's such a great story or because the film scared the wits out of either of you. In terms of the time of day, you don't want to be watching movies so late at night that you start to think it's too late for the other to go home and so they may as well spend the night there. And finally, proximity to each other can be challenging, especially if you're a touchy feely person. It only takes one or two unintended touches to stir up the emotions and cause hormones to begin to heat up and go into overdrive.

Being cognitive of each other's personal space when alone, or even with others, can help to prevent unnecessary excitement. Also keep in mind that there will be times when being near to one another will be completely off limits with regards to sustaining your celibacy. Sometimes you will need to limit the places where you spend time together. If there is a particular place that allows you more access to the other than is helpful, this could be a place to put on your "watch out" or "off limits" list. Whether the place is public or private, physically or mentally, you must be careful to devise your use of spaces so that they have the least potential of stirring up your hormones to the point where your celibacy walk may be in danger.

68: Limit/Cut Out the Guy Stories

Whether it's the ability to play sports, drive the perfect car, or any other area that reflects a man's ability or status, there is an open door of competition for men to walk right into. In most areas, competition is not a big deal at all, except when it comes to the topic of sex. When you speak on the subject of sex, you give it energy to grow and the power to try and convince you that you need it in your life. For anyone who is currently on the path of celibacy, sex talk with the guys should be totally and completely off limits.

Just as women do, men like to talk and brag about encounters that they have with the opposite sex. For men, this is one of those major areas of competition where they can get the accolades and be the envy of their friends. The hotter and more desirable the woman is to other men, the more points the man who has been with her will get. To prevent this game of who can one-up the other, your best bet is to not even participate in the game. No we're not saying that you need to chuck your innate male competitive gene or nature, but we do suggest limiting the talk to safe areas. Safe areas of topics are any areas that don't involve sex in any form.

I know you're thinking that men cannot *not* talk about sex. I'm here to tell you that *yes*, you can. When the subject of sex comes up, and we all know that it will, change the subject or leave the area and return when the subject returns to topics outside of sex. This may seem a little uncomfortable at first, but it's all designed to help you be successful in your celibacy walk with as minimal negative influences as possible.

69: <u>Move</u> the TV and Stereo Out of the Bedroom

If you're a man who likes to entertain women in the realm of your bedroom, even if it's just watching TV or listening to music, it's time to redecorate your home. This type of setup is geared toward the objective of getting a woman into bed. As you begin to change the way that you view women with respect to sex, you also need to make changes in every area of your life that could cause you to fail in your walk.

Now I know some of you will say you have your apartment set up this way because space is at a premium or it's just more convenient for you to arrange your furnishings in this way. I say it's just an excuse to keep you in a world of pre-marital sex. However, if you live in an efficiency where you have say 500, or fewer square feet in your home, the décor issue is easy to solve. Don't bring women to your apartment. This way you can keep your stereo and TV in your bedroom with no threat of the setting enticing you to go against your will of being a man who successfully walks in celibacy.

This setup doesn't apply to every man. There may be other things in your apartment or home that can cause you to be susceptible to giving into the flesh. Whatever it is, it's time to correct it. If you're not sure if such a setting exists in your home, take a moment to review your home from the eyes of when you were walking in the flesh. As you do this, think about past encounters. Look at the way that you have your furniture set up, pictures displayed, or anything that made it a little easier to set the mood for sex. Then change it. Rearrange items or remove them to an area not to be seen by any other guest in your home.

70: Limit <u>Alone Time</u> with Female Friends

This should be an easy one, but it still needs to be said. You don't need to limit your alone time with *all* female friends, only those who have seen you nude or have the potential to. Some men and women can still remain friends following sexual encounters and be able to not return to that aspect of their relationship. Although for some this is true, for others it's not. To be on the safe side, don't even acquiesce to being in a position that could potentially land you on the wrong side of the celibacy coin.

Say there is a woman that you are friends with and you've thought about maybe once or twice being sexually intimate with, but never pursued it. During a particularly rough time during your walk, circumstances bring the two of you together and your mind starts to wander a bit. Given the opportunity of alone time with this woman you can find yourself in a compromising situation that you needn't be in, if you monitor the amount of alone time you have with women.

The best rule of thumb is to engage with women in group-settings whenever possible. When you're in a relationship with a woman this can be a little more difficult and certainly more important to institute. By nature of being a couple, the two of you want and need to spend time together to build and grow the relationship. In this case, make sure that your walk is strong when you spend alone time with your lady. During the times that your strength isn't as strong, it may be best to begin to schedule alone time for another time when you are stronger. For more suggestions on being a successfully celibate couple be sure to read Section IV for helpful tips.

71: <u>Don't Make</u>/Answer the Booty Calls

We've all made or received them, male and female. Sometimes it starts out innocent enough, as a phone call to see what someone is up to. It's harmless. We're bored or a little lonely and want someone to talk to so we pick up the phone and dial a number; no objective, no goal in mind, you're just talking. Now if somewhere in the conversation there's an invitation to pay the other a visit, what's the harm in that? You're just being friendly, right? Wrong! You know exactly what you're doing and know exactly what it is that you wanted when you picked up that phone at 11:30 p.m. or later.

You thought that conversation would get you through this hard time and you'd be okay and you'd go to sleep. After talking for a while you decide to end the call and try to go to sleep. Only now, you're lonelier and more sexually riled up than ever. You're tossing and turning and beginning to think that you are in dire need. You either don't want to self relieve the sexual tension that's building inside you, or you do and it's not enough. Now you only want more. You know she's up because you just hung up, and based on the conversation you just had, chances are good that she'd welcome you into her home or would be willing to come to yours. Now you're in trouble, all because of what you thought, or tried to convince yourself, was a simple phone call.

Save yourself the trouble and don't call past 10 p.m. Any phone calls past this hour is entering into the realm of the booty call. There's nothing that needs to be said at 10 p.m. or later that can't be said earlier in the day. Calls this late also show a lack of respect for a woman. Unless a woman expressly tells you it's okay to call her after 10 p.m., air on the side of caution and respect. My father gave me this piece of advice years ago, and I still hold this as a standard today. If a man calls me after 10 p.m., and hasn't gotten an advance okay to do so, chances are great that he won't be talking to me that night. If it's a man I just met, he certainly won't be talking to me at all that night!

Remember, the time of night that a man calls a woman shows the level of respect he has for her. As a man, you may not see it this way. Women with standards will definitely see it as a sign of respect, or lack thereof. Oh, and the late night booty texts are off limits too!

72: Find Other Outlets of <u>Release</u>

The most typical outlet for a man trying to abstain from sex is to practice self-pleasure. For some men this can take the edge off. For others, it could just ignite their desire and make remaining celibate that much more difficult. The best answer I can give you in this area is the same as I did in Section I regarding the topic of sex toys. This is a decision that you have to make within yourself. Some people will say that self-pleasure is completely off limits because it reminds you of past times, or entices you to create fantasies for a future rendezvous. There are those that also feel that self-pleasure is a form of sin. Bottom line is to talk it over with God and let Him, and your spirit, direct your path as to proceed or not proceed with self-pleasure.

There are ways to relieve sexual tension without having sex. Some men use exercise for this very reason. Spend time learning a new hobby or skill, something that will take a lot of mind power; that will physically exhaust you to the point where you have little to no energy to even think about or engage in sex. Yes, I am aware that it has been said that men think about sex a great majority of their day. This may be true, but the key is to occupy your mind and control the urges through the use of mind control.

The mind is stronger than any other organ in the body. This is how some have made millions of dollars teaching the laws of attraction, which is nothing more than controlling the mind and allowing the mind to dictate your destiny. Use your mind to help you find other methods of release and you will be that much more successful in your celibacy walk.

73: Stay **Busy**

Whatever it is that you choose to do to keep your mind and body busy (outside of sex) will be another way for you to maintain your goal of being celibate. The point here is to keep busy and to reduce idle time. You've heard the saying idle hands are the devil's workshop. There is a reason why this saying has lasted through the years. It's because it is true. When you have nothing to occupy your time or your mind, you start wondering. Things that have no business in the mind seem to seek you out and find you waiting.

The devil does not want you to follow God and to walk in His ways because then you become a soul that he has lost. He is going to look for every opportunity to find a way into your mind and corrupt your thoughts. Therefore, it is crucial that you constantly keep watch over your mind. The best way to do that is to stay busy. But don't get busy just for busy sake; make it count. The best way to get and stay busy is through working on your relationship with God. In addition, there is working in the church via the choir, ushering, teaching a class, or any number of other ministries in the church.

Take a cooking class. This way you'll never go hungry; you won't need to rely on others to provide you with great meals and you'll impress women with your culinary skills. Take a dancing class. Several male athletes have done it on reality shows like "*Dancing with the Stars*" and, in the process, have made it a much "cooler" thing to do. You'll get great exercise from it and it'll open the door to meeting new people because they like the way you dance. Depending on how well you dance, it could also become another stream of income for you, by providing dance lessons to those wanting to learn from you.

I have a friend who does Chicago Stepping and many people know and gravitate toward him because of the way he dances. Because he has spent a great deal of time honing his skill at dancing, his confidence has increased. Anywhere he goes, he steals the show and is assured that he'll have a great time dancing. He's also been known to make a few extra dollars giving lessons.

You could do some work around the house, start a garden, or build something from scratch like a deck on your home or something smaller. Have you ever thought that you were an expert in a certain area and you wanted to share your knowledge? Here's a golden opportunity to do some consulting. Maybe you desire to write a book on a given subject. This is an excellent way to stay busy and to give back to others at the same time. The opportunities are numberless. So find something you enjoy and get busy staying busy.

74: <u>Pray</u>, Pray, and Pray Some More

We've supplied you with many ways and tactics to help you on your journey of celibacy. Some of these will be easier than others to implement, but they are all designed to help you in the different stages that you'll go through in your celibacy walk from being easy to a lot of hard work. But the best weapon we can provide you with in this war against pre-marital sex is to pray, pray, and pray some more. Then pray again.

There may be times when you have tried everything here outlined previously and you still aren't able to maintain. The only answer available to you at this point is prayer. Remove yourself from all outside sources and people. Get in your prayer closet and put your face to the ground, humble yourself and pray. Give it all over to God. He is there to help you through whatever it is that you need to survive in this journey, and life overall. God knows that there will be times when you feel like you can't go another step down this path, that your feet will not function to carry you on.

He already knows this. He's God. In this time, all He's looking for you to do is to turn toward Him in prayer and hand it over to Him. Let Him walk with you, or even carry you to that point where your legs will stand again, and escort you in your celibacy walk. Yolanda Adams sings a song, *"In The Midst Of It All,"* that speaks to this very thing, of how God loves, protects and will keep you in the midst of whatever you're going through, including the many temptations that you will face on this walk. Don't forsake the power and the love of God by thinking that you are man and therefore, strong enough to handle it all on your own. If that were indeed the case, then God would have never sent His son Jesus to the cross to die for all of our sins.

God would have simply said that we were strong enough on our own, and if we weren't then that was just too bad for us. He would have said that men needed to buck up and handle their own affairs. But He didn't! He never left us alone and He sent us a comforter because He knew that we would need His help. He delights in helping His children. And you became His child when you accepted Him into your life. Like any good father, God will allow us to try and find our own way, but He will always be sitting there watching and waiting to jump in when we need Him.

Because He does respect you as a man and knows the power and strength that resides within you, He will not jump in *every* time He sees you stumble. But if He doesn't jump in, He will soften the blow. If you stumble or are about to stumble and you call out to Him, He will be there before you can finish the thought. He will be there to help, support and guide you in the right direction, especially when the direction is one that He has requested you to go in. The way that you ask for His help is through prayer. You already know this; this is nothing new to you. Don't forsake the help that God is providing to you. Do not *not* go to Him when you need Him. If you want to make it successfully through this journey, then you need to pray, pray and pray some more.

One final thing to keep in mind though, there will be occasions when you will fail. God already knows this too. Sometimes you may fail totally due to your own fault, and sometimes it's due to God allowing you to do so. He won't cause you to fail, but He may allow you to fail, especially during those times when you chose to go your own way versus seeking His help. This is not meant to punish you or to discourage you, but to help you learn from your mistakes. It's to show you that all of this could have been prevented by turning to Him and asking Him for His Help.

Popular TV pastor Joel Osteen told a story in one of his broadcasts of some friends visiting their home with their children. One of the kids was particularly energetic and didn't like to listen when adults told him not to do something. It was Christmas time and the Osteens had this beautiful tree up that drew the child's attention. Joel told of how his wife was nervous that the child would turn the tree over on himself if he didn't leave it alone. The whole time the father of the child was just as calm as the Osteens were nervous. Joel asked the father if he didn't he see his child misbehaving and wondered why he was so calm. The father acknowledged that he did see him and stated that he would let him keep at it. He indicated that he could tell the child not to do something and he wouldn't listen. But when the tree falls on him, he wouldn't have to tell him again not to do something because his son will have learned his lesson. So you know what happened. The tree fell over on the boy and the father was right. From that moment on he didn't have to tell his son anything twice again. His son knew that when daddy says something, it's probably best to listen.

The same thing occurs with God. It's not that the father (in the story above) didn't love his son; he just knew that that was a lesson his son had to learn on his own. He knew the next time his son was on the verge of getting into trouble that maybe he'd stop and think about the consequences. Chances are the son would look to the father for his help or guidance before going down the wrong path again. The son wouldn't have learned that lesson without the tree falling on him. He wasn't open to hearing from his father, even though the father was sitting right there to guide him. God is sitting right there ready to guide you, you just need to ask Him for His help. You just need to pray your way through and you too can prevent that proverbial tree from falling upon you.

75: Go to <u>Sleep</u>

Sleep is a wonderful thing. Believe it or not, it's a wonderful tool in the journey of celibacy. In order for it to be effective though, you must couple it with prayer. I initially included this in Section II for women, but it works so well for either sex, that I also included it here in Section III.

I know men that have used this tactic and will swear by its power. It's really simple. You already know the power of prayer and its benefits in your life. You already know what a good night's sleep will do for you. Add them together and you are off to a peaceful night with your celibacy intact. You live to fight and add another day to your success. When you've tried other options to curb your hormones and desires, try saying a prayer and then going straight to sleep. The prayer can be long and in-depth, or it can be quick and short. The only real requirement is that your prayer proceeding sleep must be heartfelt; it must be sincere. That's it!

Say a quick prayer asking God to grant you strength in staying faithful in your commitment to Him, to be celibate, and then go to sleep. You can be in the middle of doing something or making plans to go against your vow when you stop, say a prayer and go to sleep. There is no set amount of time that you need to sleep. It can be a few moments or it can be for an extended sum of time. The goal of sleep is for you to distract and divert the mind and your hormones from the thoughts and effects of sexual intercourse. That's not to say that when you wake that all feelings and desires will have disappeared. But they will have lessened enough for you to continue on and not lose your celibacy. So say a prayer, take a nap and keep it movin'.

SECTION IV

For the Single Couple

At this point in the process of being celibate, one of three things is in play for you. You are a new single couple, you're an existing single couple or you are preparing yourself for when you become a single couple. Now that you've reached this final section of the book, you have gained a foundation in celibacy from Section I that has given you a great start. In Sections II and III you've formed building blocks on the road of celibacy that have been geared toward your particular sex. You've been enlightened to some of the challenges that the other sex faces and tools that can aid them in their successful journey as a single, unattached, celibate adult. This final section discusses how to take what you've learned in Sections I through III as a single celibate adult and apply those lessons to being a single celibate couple.

Remember, even though you may be in a relationship with someone, you are still single. Unless you have exchanged wedding vows in a ceremony performed by an authorized official, you are still single. So don't be confused, you should still be abstaining from any form of sexual intercourse. You do not get a pass because you promise to be monogamous and only sleep with the person that you are in a relationship with. It's also not about being celibate only when you're a solo single. Being in a relationship doesn't constitute permission to start having sex. If you believe that it does, I am here to tell you – wrong answer! This section is designed to help you continue your celibacy, while being a participant in a relationship. Your dating status may have changed, but your celibacy status hasn't.

Being honest with you again, it is a lot easier to be a celibate single than it is to be a celibate couple. I've mentioned previously that my longest consistent and successful vow of celibacy was six years long. I sincerely believe that I was able to accomplish those six years due, in large part, to being a solo single. Had I been a part of a couple, I don't believe I would have been as successfully celibate for the full six years. I say this because in order to be with someone for that long and not have sex in the picture, you have to really be invested in the relationship. There has to be love pouring out from every facet of each of your beings, or that neither of you have any semblance of a sex drive whatsoever. You have to really love the person and the things that make them who they are, the good and the bad. If you don't, chances are the relationship either won't last long or won't be very fulfilling, that is if it is intended to be a romantic relationship.

When sex is a part of a relationship and it is very enjoyable, people have a tendency to stay longer than they probably would if sex were not part of the relationship. What am I saying? I'm saying that great sex will make a person put up with something or someone longer than they probably should. Simply because the sex is amazing or mind blowing and they don't want to lose that good feeling because they don't know if they'll find it with the next person. If the person is bored and the sex is okay, again they will stay around a little longer than they may prefer to until something better comes along.

If you want to know how strong your relationship is and exactly how much your partner loves and cares about you, then try removing sex from the picture and you will get your answer quickly! If the answer isn't positive, then maybe you might want to consider returning to being a solo single. If the answer *is* positive, you might want to think about taking this relationship to the next level. Use this test to guide the steps in your relationship and to move the relationship forward with the confidence that you are with the right person and on the right path to a happy and successful journey of celibacy. This road will usher you into a happy and successful marriage because you've taken the time to learn about and appreciate one another in a way that you may not have experienced had you not taken this journey. Let's get started!

76: **Right Person/<u>Right</u> Reasons**

Do you know someone that regardless of how long ago you last saw them, they are always in a relationship with someone new? This is what we call a serial dater, people who can't seem to function unless they are in a relationship with someone else. We all know someone like this or have been that person. But at some point in life, if you want a lasting and meaningful relationship you have to stop jumping from person to person and take the time to get to know someone to see if you two are an ideal fit for each other. There are many people who believe that there is only one true love or true soul mate; that there's only one person designed especially for them. There are others that believe that there can be many "true loves" in one's life, and that there is no perfect person for anyone. They simply see someone as perfect for the moment or that that person possesses a set of values or standards required for a happy life.

If you're looking to be in a lasting relationship, then you need to begin evaluating the person that you're with to determine if this is the right person for you, or if they're the right person for right now. There's nothing wrong with being with someone and not having an intention to expand the relationship into more, if you both agree that that is what you both want out of the relationship. But if something has changed for either of you, then it is time to reevaluate the person that you are with at that moment and the relationship as a whole. As human beings we grow and experience life and various events in our own world and the world around us on a constant and continual basis. Each of those elements will leave some imprint that will add small or large layers to who we are and ultimately to what we want in life. As this occurs it's important to conduct regular checkups of your relationship. You do this to make sure everything is working well and to catch anything that can potentially become an issue down the road.

It's not that you're looking for issues to arise. You're doing preventative maintenance in the same way that you should be getting an annual physical with your primary physician or a biannual cleaning and exam with your dentist. When you're not taking these measures into account on a regular basis, you waste time and energy down the road, trying to rectify a major issue that was once small or could have been prevented in the first place. By simply taking the time to make sure you are in the right situation with the right person, you're establishing yourself for success. When it comes to your celibacy walk you need to do the same thing. Evaluate the relationship that you're currently in and the person that is in it with you. In order for both of you to be a successful celibate couple, you both need to be on the same page as to where you are and where you're going.

For many couples they will come together as two celibate adults or they will make the choice to move from a sexual relationship to a non-sexual relationship. Regardless of how you two get there, it is important that you still have the discussion to determine if you're right for each other and that you are on the same plan. One person's concept of celibacy may be different from the other person and this needs to be known from the start. You may discover that you are both on the same page and paragraph in terms of walking in celibacy. But you may find that you're years or miles apart in many other areas of your relationship and what constitutes an ideal future.

Or the reverse could be true in that you find that you are in alignment in many areas but are not equal in your celibacy walk. For example, one half of the relationship might believe in being celibate until the point where you two become engaged. The other half might believe in being celibate until the official words of "you are now husband and wife" have been pronounced and marriage licenses have been signed (as is defined in the Bible and throughout the pages of this book). Knowing this upfront prevents issues later down the road.

As you begin to walk as a celibate couple and make changes in your relationship to line up with your goals, make sure to spend serious time in thought and conversation understanding how living in celibacy will change the relationship and the participants within it. Put in the work to get you both on the same page. Taking on the path of celibacy is not just about the physical act of sex. That is but a small part of the journey.

The largest part of this change is reshaping the way that you both think and behave overall in your life and in your relationship. You're not signing up for a lifetime without sex. You're signing up for a life of respecting your spirit, respecting your partner; of rearranging your priorities and assigning sex its appropriate place in your unmarried coupled life.

77: Keep <u>God First</u> in Your Relationship

The saying "the family that prays together, stays together" has survived for many generations because it holds true. This is true because those families realize that life is bigger than them and that they require the assistance of God in their lives to be whole and at peace with love and joy. Those families recognize that the driving force and support system in their life is the love and guidance of God. Those families also understand that in order to be successful they must lean on God to help them in their present and future lives. They know that they must turn to God daily for His direction and guidance as to the ways that they should go. These families consult with God when making decisions for they know He will lead them down the right path.

Blessed is the man who listens to me, watching daily at my gates, waiting at the posts of my doors. For whoever finds me finds life, and obtains favor from the Lord;

–Proverbs 8:34-35

If you are a couple that has God as the third member of your relationship, you already know the power that He has in your current situation. Now that you've decided to add celibacy as the fourth component in your relationship, you will find that you will need Him more at this point in the relationship than you have in the past. However, if your current relationship only consists of the two of you and you decide to add the third element of celibacy into it, I would very highly recommend that you add God into the relationship as well. As you join together or continue on as a couple, make sure that God is not only in the midst of your relationship, but at the head of the relationship.

78: Have the <u>Discussion</u>

Whether you're just beginning the relationship or have been together for a period of time, it is important to have the celibacy discussion. If you were both celibate before coming together, you each had your own method of maintaining your celibacy. Now that you're together, the methods that you used as single celibates will differ from the methods that you'll use as a celibate couple. In Section II we talk about not allowing men into your home, as this can be an open doorway to getting yourself into trouble. But as a couple, spending time alone with each other is crucial to building the relationship and establishing trust. Determining how much time that you spend together and when it's not appropriate to be alone together are a few of the topics that need to be discussed as you enter into this new realm of celibacy together. Being a newly formed couple will make it a bit easier to have this discussion than it will be for an established couple. This is because sex was previously not a part of your relationship, where it probably was as an established couple.

When people are in new a relationship they tend to be cautious and don't want to rock the boat. They are still feeling their way around the other person and may fear the results of some of the limitations that they may propose to the other. Most people don't want to come across as too demanding or bossy, so something that may need to be said at the onset of a relationship may not be, with the goal of bringing it up at a later time. This is what can make it hard.

The beginning of a relationship is the perfect time to discuss your expectations because you are not set in your relationship ways and habits. People are more willing to please and accommodate their partner when the energy is new and exciting. This is usually at the start of the relationship. Because you are learning each other's habits and behaviors, making your needs and wants known are simply that -- your needs and wants. They are not viewed as demands or attempts to change the other person. It's like starting a new job. You and your new employer sit down and discuss the terms that will allow you to become a part of that company. You and your partner will do the same and discuss each of your wants and needs and come to an agreement of what it will take for you two to have a healthy and happy relationship.

For those couples that decide to shift their relationship and practice celibacy until they marry, the change is going to be more significant as you've already established a mode and means of communicating with one another that involves sexual intercourse. For some couples, this is a very large portion of their communication and they now need to learn how to better communicate verbally and non-verbally (excluding sex). Partners who used the excuse of not being a good communicator will now have to toss that excuse out the window and get to work improving on their communication skills. This can be accomplished through games, role-play and a variety of other methods.

One of the good things about shifting your relationship is that your relationship now becomes new and exciting again in ways that it has never been. You are learning new ways to please each other and to express your love. You are building your intimacy to greater and deeper levels. You are learning new things about the other that you may never have known, had you two not taken this journey together. You are also learning new and different things about yourself. You're learning what you want, what you need and how you can give more to your partner and to others. If there was an area of change in your own life that you've been stalling on, this is a great opportunity to implement it while you're currently in a mode of change and adjustment. These are all goods things and are all part of improving your overall relationship.

Another key factor about having this discussion and the resulting change that comes about is that it shows you both who you are as individuals, and as a couple. Becoming celibate as a point of discussion may sound like a great idea to you both. But as an actual act, it can be too much for some people to undertake and to shift their relationship in that direction. If this happens in your relationship, you may want to look at other areas of your relationships and see if there are more areas that you two are not compatible in. If this is the case, it may be better to end things now rather than later down the road when your lives are much more entangled.

Now before we go any further, let me be clear about one thing here. In no way am I advocating breaking up relationships for the sake of breaking up. What I am trying to convey is that making such a large change as moving toward living a celibate life is about much more than a physical change. We've stated this throughout this book and will state it again. The change to celibacy is about a mental, emotional, spiritual *and* a physical change. It does not just impact your sexual life, but every part of your life. It is a life-altering change. In order to be successfully celibate, you must change and renew your mind and your way of thinking. You must adjust your emotional being and get into better alignment with your spiritual/religious self. These changes are life altering; there is no way around it. You cannot walk in celibacy and not be changed internally.

When you make a change, such as this one, you'd better expect that there is going to be some tension. Even if the tension is only minor and/or for a short period of time, it is going to happen and it is going to affect your relationship. Pay attention to your partner and how they handle it and how the relationship continues. You may just find that this change is too much for the relationship to bear. If this is the case, then you know that maybe the relationship isn't as strong as you thought it was and that maybe it's time to move on. We're not saying that it will happen, but just be prepared in case it does.

79: **Take the Vow <u>Together</u>**

Now that you've had the discussion and decided to become a celibate couple from a spiritual, mental and emotional standpoint, it's time to talk about it from a physical point of view. So what does celibacy mean in terms of couples? Let's talk about what it does and does not mean so there is no ambiguity.

Being celibate means that you do not engage in sexual intercourse in any form, including oral sex, inside or outside of the relationship. Being celibate means that you don't caress each other's sensual body parts to the point of no return. Being celibate means that it's probably not a good idea to spend the night together in the same bed. Celibacy means that you don't use sex toys with or on each other as this can lead to other things and sexual intercourse taking place. Celibacy means that you don't watch pornographic films together for the same reason. Being celibate means that you don't tempt, taunt and entice each other.

Being celibate does mean finding other ways to show your love to your partner. Being celibate means growing the intimacy in the relationship outside of the bedroom. Celibacy means that you take the other person's feelings into consideration when they're having a hard time maintaining their vow. Celibacy means still having a physical relationship, but one with limits. The limits that the two of you, as a couple, place upon yourselves are up to your discretion. Just keep in mind that you know each other's triggers and what it takes to get the other going. Use this knowledge wisely and don't be afraid to use physical space and distance as tools to help keep you both successful in your walk. There will be times that you need to spend time apart to keep the journey moving forward. As long as you communicate with each other on a regular basis you are more apt to succeed.

Now you're all set. You've had the discussion and made the decision to be a celibate couple. You understand some of the dos and don'ts that will help you along the path. Now the only thing left to do is to take the vow together. Make it an event. Have a party, a romantic dinner or any way that you choose to celebrate. Set a date and time and make it special. You can prepare a few words in advance explaining to the other what this means to you both or you can simply speak from the heart. Make it a ceremony. It doesn't have to be big or grand, it can be short and sweet. Just make it special and unique to the two of you. Go to www.kamasutraofcelibacy.com and print out the *Covenant Pledge of Celibacy for Couples* and sign it just as you would a marriage certificate and begin your journey!

80: Engage in <u>Counseling</u>

Counseling has many wonderful benefits from helping one to alleviate negative emotions to preparing a couple to enter into a healthy relationship together. Many people believe counseling or therapy to mean that there is something severely wrong with them or fear that others would look at them differently. This couldn't be further from the truth. If you have a major toothache that is not helped by home remedies and becomes infected, it is in your best interest to go and see a dentist before the issue becomes worse and you possibly lose a tooth or two.

Let's look at it from the other end of the spectrum. You're in fairly good health and know that you could be doing better by seeking the assistance of a nutritionist who will design an overall eating plan that can improve your health, increase your energy and reshape your waistline. In either of these scenarios would you think it odd of yourself for getting help? Do you think that others will look at you as if there is something really wrong with you for seeking help in these areas? The answer is no, absolutely not!

The same holds true with counseling. If there is an area in your life where you need help or can be better in, why not seek the aid and assistance to help you to be successful in that area. Pick up any college or community center catalogue and you will find classes from basket weaving, to belly dancing to the study of bugs or dealing with grief and more. But there are little to no classes on how to be successful in a relationship. There are tons of books and articles on improving your relationship but not many sessions or classes where you can interact with an instructor or with other couples sharing the same experiences. In many religions, when a couple decides to marry, there are pre-marital classes. These classes could last for a few weeks to a month or two. They will offer the couple guidance as they begin the next phase of their life.

Wouldn't it be more helpful to have had these types of classes at the start of your relationship? Think of some of the issues you experienced in your past relationships and the things that you learned when it was all over. Many of us walk away more knowledgeable, at the end of the relationship, about who we are as individuals. We learn lessons that we can utilize in our next relationship. But how many of us actually use them? Your intentions may be good, but that may not be enough. Now throw celibacy into the relationship and you're dealing with a whole new dimension of complexity.

Being celibate can be challenging as a solo single, but it can be even more so as a single couple. If you're willing to take the vow together and live the life, why not add in a few sessions of counseling to help you two navigate the waters, especially in the beginning of the relationship or during the shift to celibacy. Some couples are great at communicating with one another while others struggle in this area. There may be times during your walk together where tensions will increase due to the lack of sex. One or both of you may feel like you've lost a major outlet, as those tensions would have normally been released through sex. So how do you deal with this?

A great start would be counseling. Counseling doesn't just involve talking; it also includes exercises and techniques to help you deal with the stress of not having sex in the relationship. In addition, counseling can teach you new ways to communicate with one another. The benefits you can gain are endless. Consider adding a few sessions of couples counseling into your relationship as you walk the path of celibacy and watch how it improves the relationship. Just make sure that the counselor shares the same values in terms of celibacy and waiting until marriage. If they don't, they will have a harder time understanding why sex is not a part of the relationship and in turn, won't be as effective as one who does share your belief.

81: Keep Others Out of <u>Your Business</u>

Aside from a couple's therapist or counselor, one of the best tools you can have as a couple on your celibacy journey is to keep others out of your relationship. This is important for any relationship, but even more so for celibate couples. Say as a woman you did something awful and you don't know how to tell your partner because you know how upset he's going to be. You talk it over with one of your girlfriends and ask for advice on how to tell him. Depending on how big the issue is she may suggest an evening where you wear something sexy and give him a night to remember. You remind her of the vow of celibacy that you two have taken. She tells you that yes that's important but you need to make it up to him in a big way and you can always start again in your celibacy walk.

You're a man who has been under a tremendous amount of stress and have a great deal of tension and pent up energy. Your current methods of release aren't working. You talk to your male friends about it and ask for suggestions. Chances are they'll say something to the effect of it being a result of a lack of sex and will more than likely encourage you to go get you some (sex) and relieve the pressure. As they "counsel" you, if they're not on the same path of celibacy as yourself, they will undoubtedly steer you in the wrong direction.

In both scenarios your friends mean well. Their intentions are good, but misguided. But there are still other situations where others can steer you wrong. A friend or a family member who doesn't understand or agree with what you're doing may tell you that it is unnatural to be in a relationship without the presence of sex. A common theme will be that you won't be able to keep your partner without satisfying their sexual needs. They will tell you that there is someone else out there who is more than willing to do what your partner won't. Truth is, they're right, partially. There are other people out there who would be willing to satisfy your partner, or even yourself, sexually, if allowed the opportunity. But if you and your partner are both committed to each other and your vow of celibacy, with the techniques and ideas presented here in this book, a great support system, couple's counseling, prayer and the grace of God, you can and will walk into your new life of celibacy, and beyond, with success. The key is to bring the right people into the relationship (those supporting your goal), and to keep those who have shown themselves as non-supportive, out of your relationship.

82: Establish the Rules/Set <u>Boundaries</u>

Establishing a set of rules to live by in general and in your relationships is paramount to ensuring that you are being loved, respected and maintaining dignity within yourself and with others. For each person, these rules and boundaries will differ. They don't have to be many, or extensive in nature, but they should be something of substance to you and who you are and who you're striving to be. These rules are designed to protect you from neglect and misuse. They are also there to encourage and drive you forward to your desired goals and accomplishments. In earlier sections, we talked a lot about guarding your borders and watching those that you let into your life. We talked about people that will help to keep you in forward movement and those who understand the importance of your goals. There are many who are great in this area and do it in every relationship; every one but the love relationship. So we want to make sure to take time to give attention to this area, especially when it comes to living a celibate life in a romantic relationship.

For some people, their boundaries and rules are a little gentler than some others. Rules are set, put into play and displayed to those whom they are involved with. The key is to find out what works for you and then go with it. Part of learning how to set your rules and boundaries is to know who you are and to be true to yourself and about your strengths and weaknesses. Let me give you an example. I abstain from sex because my spirit rakes me raw when I don't. I feel like such a disappointment to God and myself when I go against my celibacy vow. For me, having sex outside of marriage is pleasing to my body and damaging to my soul, mind and spirit. It's three against one and I always lose when I allow all parts of my being to experience the encounter of sexual intercourse. For this reason, and the fact that my flesh can be very weak and given the right state of mind and circumstances I can potentially fail, my rules are much stricter than some others would be.

I have friends who are less tempted physically than I am and their rules are lighter. An example of this is residential space. I do not enter a man's home or allow men to enter mine unless I know that I am not his type (nor is any woman). Now this is not to say that I can't control myself sexually, because I can. It is to say that I don't desire to be tempted in this way. For me to enter a man's home or for he to enter mine, it is because we are involved in a relationship and have a great deal of chemistry and some sense of intimacy. If this is not in place, we don't cross thresholds. This is part of the rules that I set up for myself.

On the other hand, I have friends who are celibate who will enter a man's home but will establish their rules by the seating that they choose. One friend told me about a visit to a man's house where he had a single chair and a loveseat in his home. She immediately took the solo chair and left him on the cozy sofa. This was her method of establishing boundaries and letting the man know her rules. Determine what your boundaries are and make them known.

The thing to remember is that there will be times when you are tempted.

But each one is tempted when he is drawn away by his own desires and enticed.

–James 1:14

Temptation will not take a holiday because you have decided to become celibate. In fact, it will be notified that you are trying to live for God in this area of your life and will bombard you with many opportunities to convert you back to a sexual world. Just remember that although you will be tempted, if you make an effort to put your boundaries in place from the very beginning, you can and will withstand the test. In the end, God will reward your efforts of resisting temptation (you do this by establishing and enacting your boundaries).

Blessed is the man who endures temptation; for when he has been approved, he will receive the crown of life which the Lord has promised to those who love Him.

–James 1:12

For couples that are more involved in their relationship, their rules will differ even further. In these relationships you are building intimacy outside the realm of sex. You may need to feel the physical closeness of sitting beside each other and holding hands or even touching each other. This is fine, as long as there are boundaries established long before you get to this point as to how far you can go and what happens when things get a bit heated. Establish a code word, a look, or something that can be easily conveyed to both of you to mean that maybe you need to part physically to regain your composure.

For some couples this may mean that the evening needs to come to an end. Kiss and say good night. Your communication can still continue via phone, Skype, instant message or texting. It doesn't mean contact with one another ends for the night, but that the physical proximity does end so that each of you can clear your head and regain strength. The key is to set the boundaries and rules from the very start of the relationship and plan the escape routes to help you both maintain your celibacy.

Discuss them in the beginning and throughout the relationship as one or both of you may have changed a bit during the natural course of the relationship. Some things that may have been okay at the start may not be okay now or are too hard or not strict enough for your current state. Keep the lines of communication open and be flexible with each other and the needs of both, and you will continue to be successful in your celibacy journey.

83: Build a Bond of <u>Trust</u> and <u>Respect</u>

In order for every relationship to be nourished and to grow, a bond of trust needs to be in place. Part of building that bond of trust is giving and receiving respect, providing an environment in which it can grow. Each party needs to feel and believe that they can trust the other with their thoughts, feelings and overall being. This is what a covenant is. As a celibate couple, I encourage you to sign the *Covenant Pledge of Celibacy for Couples* as part of your celibacy walk together. But even beyond the pledge, you need to be able to have a strong bond of trust and respect with the person you're involved in the relationship with. When this bond is absent, jealousy may exist and problems arise. Just note that trust is something that is earned and built over time through actions and words substantiated with corresponding movement. For some, trust is a handshake. For others, it's created over an evening of drinks and dinner. Unfortunately, none of these actions truly constitute trust; they are illusions.

Imagine that there is a new parking structure being built and you have a front seat view of it from your office window. You see the construction workers pushing the dirt on the ground back and forth, smoothing it out. Over the next week they bring in steel posts and begin constructing the levels. After a week of work, the parking structure is open for business. You've witnessed every step of the building process and nowhere in this process did you ever see an actual foundation being dug and poured. The steel posts are not cemented into the ground and are being supported by some above ground measures. The builder has stated that the parking garage is safe for use.

How long is it going to take before the structure falls and crumbles? How many vehicles can enter before the structure begins to sway and collapse? The builder has certified in words that it is safe but has provided no visual or concrete proof that the structure is safe. This is what it looks like when you lack a foundation of trust in your relationship. You hear the words, but there are no actions to support it. There is no cement put into place. You can't build a safe multi-tiered structure in a week without an adequate foundation, nor can you build a relationship or bond of trust merely with words. It takes time and patience. It takes evidence to prove what has been stated is in fact what has occurred or is occurring. If at the beginning of a celibate relationship you see a building going up quickly with no foundation being poured, that's a red flag that the foundation (trust) will be an issue and it may be best to just move on before investing any more time.

I had a recent experience of meeting a man and spending an evening with him over dinner. The chemistry was okay; we talked about the work we both did; and we both enjoyed the evening. Prior to us actually meeting for the date he knew I had been writing this book on celibacy. During the date he mentioned sex being a big part of a relationship and that going without it would be hard, but he was willing to try. We spoke of seeing each other again and ended the night. The next day I received a text from him stating:

"Two people holding each other close, listening to the rain. Nice."
My response was, *"Sounds nice."*
He: *"So."*
Me: *"And."*
He: *"Your place or mine?"*
Me: *"I don't do places."*

The texting continued on for a while and finally ended with me proposing a compromise of offering to meet him somewhere. He responded with, *"It's storming out!"* Normally, based on my standards, I would be finished with a gentleman at this point and have nothing further to do with him. Realizing that maybe he was just testing my limits, I decided to give him the benefit of doubt and continued communicating with him. There was minimal communication over the next week as I was out of town. When I returned he invited me to join him in another state under the guise of getting to know each other, as he was now out of town traveling on business.

This is a perfect example of saying one thing but trying to action another. It's also an example of one trying to portray trust with someone they have only spent two hours with! When I confronted him on his intentions, he stated that there was absolutely no sexual intent, but merely a means of getting to know one another. Now if you believe this, I've got some flying monkeys I'd like to sell you. The point is this; there was not enough time for me to build any trust here. The words the gentleman spoke to my face were not in alignment with the various texts he sent me, also causing my respect for him to diminish. Because of his lack of respect for my beliefs and practice, and his attempts to force trust in himself upon me, I had no other choice but to end all communication with him. There was no room for a bond of trust or respect to even begin to be built.

As a celibate couple you really need to build the trust right from the very beginning of the relationship. Because sex is such an integral part of most relationships, the absence of it can cause greater issues of trust than in those relationships that have sex as a part of it. When you're in a celibate relationship, you may tend to wonder a bit more than usual if your partner is having sex with someone else because you are not having sex with him or her. This is why is it critical to ensure that you both are being celibate together and why you need to build a bond of trust between the two of you to help alleviate the worry and jealousy that may occur. Start the bond with a solid foundation from the very onset. If you don't, you will have an uphill battle later on in the relationship trying to establish it. Make it easy on yourselves and start off on the right foot to better achieve success in your walk of celibacy!

84: <u>Share</u> Your Secrets/Fears

So we just talked about building trust and respect in your relationship, but exactly how do you do that? One of the ways to strengthen your bond is through sharing your secrets and fears with your partner. For some, this will be fairly easy as they are an open book and love sharing their life with others. While for others, this will be quite a task. The whole purpose of expressing this portion of yourself is to open up and allow the other person to know who you are, outside of what you show the world. This is also a perfect method of building respect and trust.

There are many factors and experiences that shape who we are, what we think, and how we behave. Some of these, we are aware of their impact, and others we are not aware of until years later, if ever. As we talk about various fears and events with our partners, we sometimes discover how embedded these altering fears and secrets are in our life. And sometimes we are healed and/or relieved of some of the pressure it takes to carry them around. We all bring enough baggage into our relationships, talking with our partner about our secrets and our fears can make the load that we tote a bit lighter and pave the way for a healthier relationship.

Acknowledging your secrets and fears doesn't have to be a grand event or ceremony. It's an everyday conversation. It is a romantic night in. It's face-to-face communication. If that is too much because you can't stand to be looked at or don't want to see the reaction of the other, it can be done in a letter (written and burned after reading). Whatever it is, it starts with a word, then two, and continues on until the story is told. Your release of your secrets and fears can begin with telling an embarrassing story and work your way up to a life-altering event. It can also be done in the reverse or somewhere in the middle. The key is to start somewhere and begin building the trust in your relationship.

One important thing to keep in mind when you are on the receiving end of hearing a secret or fear is to be cautious as to how you respond to your partner and how you handle the knowledge of what you've just been told. When a person holds in a deep dark secret for many years it can be hard for them to let it go. How you respond will determine how much more is shared with you in the future and that person's perception of you. Your response will either improve the relationship or can be the start to shutting it down.

I'll give you two examples of how a response can go right and how it can go wrong. For much of my life I held such a secret and didn't share it with anyone at all. When the secret was released it was only done so within my family. The only two people I told outside my family were men I was in love with. One was Philip, who I mentioned earlier; the other was another man that at one point I was also in love with.

When I told the second man, we were driving in the car and he was taking me home. We were talking and for some reason I felt close enough to him to share this with him. Here's how his response went, "*This makes me so much more attracted to you.*" When I heard those words, I just wanted to smack the hell out of him and get out of the car. But instead, I just looked at him and thought it was the most insensitive and uncompassionate thing I had ever heard him say to me. I later found out that what he meant was that I was always guarded and didn't let him in, until that moment. When I found this out, the damage had already been done. For me, it really altered my view of him and our relationship as a whole.

When I shared my secret with Philip, it was an ordinary night. We were in his room lying across the bed watching TV and talking as we so often did. Again, I don't know how the subject came up but I found myself telling him what happened to me. His response was, "*I already knew. I just didn't know when.*" I have to tell you, I could not have loved that man any more than I had at that very moment. More importantly, he waited for me to let him know what I needed. I then found myself sharing more with him and we drew closer together. By my telling him that one secret, he understood me much better and we loved each other much more for it.

When you're in a celibate relationship you need to find other ways to connect to your partner and to grow your relationship. Sharing your secrets and fears with each other can be a great avenue to building intimacy and strengthening your celibate relationship.

85: Improve on <u>Communication</u> Daily

So often in relationships we don't communicate as effectively as we can. Many times there are hurt feelings and misunderstandings that could have been avoided and/or alleviated simply by communicating. Communication doesn't have to require a lot of time or a lot of work if done daily. The more you do it, the easier it becomes and the more you and your partner can appreciate the openness. By communicating on a regular basis you know where you and the relationship stand. When you communicate regularly, there are far less surprises when an issue is presented to the relationship because you should already be aware of it through your regular communications. At the very least, you now have a better method of dealing with it.

So what does this daily contact look like? It can be a call in the morning just to say hi. It could be a slight touch to the arm or the small of the back. A look can convey more than words strung together can ever say. There was a man I knew who, every now and then, would call and leave a message on my work phone so it was waiting for me when I arrived. He only spoke a few words, usually at the end of the message. The rest of the message was a small portion of some song to let me know that he was thinking of me.

After the first couple of calls, the message would just be the song with no additional words spoken. None were needed. When I received these messages, it always made me smile. It gave me something to look forward to at the end of the day, talking with him. Because he knew that I have such a great love of music, it gave both of us an instant means of communicating with one another. He knew this about me because we talked about our likes and dislikes.

But maybe music isn't your style of communication. That's okay. Find something that has meaning to both you and your other half and use that as your tool to communicate with each other. Take something that you love and allow it to be the catalyst to your communication. If you're a sports fan, there's a reason why you love it beyond the competitive edge and adrenaline. Use the things that you love about sports and relate it to your relationship. Say it's the teamwork and camaraderie that you enjoy. Convey that to your partner and find a way to make it a part of the relationship. An example is in the way that you have each other's back, regardless of the situation. Express to your partner how that is a quality that you admire and desire in the relationship and begin to work on it.

Even something as ordinary as cooking can be used as a different means of communication. A great example of this is the film *Like Water for Chocolate*. The entire movie is a love story told through the use of food and recipes. I once mentioned to someone I was dating how much I loved this movie. I tried to get him to watch it with me but, dismissing it as a "chick flick," he declined. However, he did tuck it away as another piece of information about me. Many months later, he was home one night flicking through the channels when he came across the movie. He watched it and understood what it was that I saw in the film and why I loved it so. He called to tell me about it and how much he enjoyed it. That film served as a point of connection and communication for us to draw closer together.

These are just a few examples of how you can take everyday things, events and daily life components to develop and build your connections with your partner on a daily basis. Because you are not having sex, you need to touch each other (spiritually, mentally and emotionally) any and every way that you can to build that intimacy in your celibate relationship. Be open to new ways of fusing with each other and to new things your partner wishes to share with you, as it may be their attempt to communicate with you in a new and fresh approach.

86: Write Each Other <u>Love</u> Letters

Writing letters is a lost art. When was the last time you wrote someone a letter, let alone a love letter? No, I don't mean a text or an email, but a handwritten letter that expresses your feelings. As children in elementary school we wrote letters with words like: "I like you. Do you like me? Check Yes or No."

Somewhere along the way to adulthood, many of us lost that innocence and freedom of expression found in writing love letters. But it doesn't have to stay lost. Imagine how you or your partner would feel to find a hand-addressed envelope among the usual stack of bills and junk mail. Many of us would be shocked and curious about its contents. To open that envelope and find a letter written from the person that you love and are in a relationship with can be a wonderful surprise. It shows your partner that you've thought a great deal of them and took some effort to show them just how much you care for them.

For those who are not used to writing love letters, I offer a few pointers. Your letter doesn't have to be long, drawn out, gushy or filled with flowery poetry. It just needs to be from the heart. Speak about things that you want or need to tell your partner. It can be something that you didn't quite know how to say in person, or a reiteration of things you've already said or done. It can be a funny joke or a moment that is shared between the two of you. The letter can be formal or informal. It can be a riddle or contain an anagram that reveals a special message. It just needs to convey your feelings and have meaning to it.

If you want to write a letter that is a heart warmer and contains romantic elements but are not sure of what to write, write song lyrics and relate it to your partner and/or your relationship. Use poetry or quote a line from a movie or favorite book. Go online or visit a bookstore or library to browse through books or websites for inspiration. If you're not good with words, try drawing a picture. If art is not your thing, draw a bunch of hearts that spells out love or some other word of meaning to you both. You could even draw a bouquet of flowers, which should be fairly easy to draw.

The key is to express your feelings and love in a different style than you normally do. If you absolutely can't think of anything else to write, think back on a great date the two of you had together or a really good conversation you had and write about your thoughts and feelings about the date or conversation. Highlight the good points that either of you made. This lets your partner know how meaningful this was to you and that you value what they had to say and share with you.

Many people use sex as a form of communication to express their love to their partner. In a celibate relationship, this is not an option. You need to find another way to accomplish the same goal. Writing love letters is but one more way to do this.

87: Develop Non-Sexual Means of <u>Intimacy</u>

Intimacy in any romantic relationship is crucial for it to flourish and to grow to its full potential. For many people the words *sex* and *intimacy* are synonymous and interchangeable when used in discussions about relationships. But this couldn't be further from the truth. Intimacy is about sharing and getting to know something or someone on a very personal and private level. It's a high level exposure to something or someone that is not readily available to anyone else or to the rest of the world. Sex is sex, it's physical; it's copulation. Sex can be a *form* of intimacy or another way to *experience* intimacy in the relationship. But it is not the only way. Because you're a celibate couple, you have to work a little more at showing and expressing your love, building your intimacy and communing with your partner, than those couples who use sex to convey all of those things. But that doesn't mean that it has to be harder. It simply means that you need to use your wits a bit more and be more creative in your approach.

In the last few topics we talked about a few ways to increase and build intimacy in a celibate relationship, but there are many other ways to accomplish the same goal. Most of the topics in this book address celibacy from the stance of the mental, emotional and the spiritual realm. Little is spoken of the physical side of being in a celibate relationship because we wanted to establish a strong and solid foundation. We wanted to build upon the other aspects of the human psyche that will be the driving force in helping you to be successful at being celibate. Now that we have that in place, let's talk a little about the physicality of being in a celibate relationship.

Because we are physical beings we must have some fashion of physical interactions in our romantic and everyday relationships. I caution you to be careful in how you go about implementing physical components into your relationship. Kissing, touching, holding, caressing and even sleeping in the same room can be fine in a celibate relationship, within reason. Go in stages, take your time with these actions and go slow. Some of these things that you did prior to being celibate was not a big deal. It was part of the romantic relationship. It can still be part of a celibate relationship but maybe not to the extent that it once was.

Previously you could lie in the same bed as your partner and not have to have sex or even think about it. Yes, it does happen occasionally! But now as a celibate adult, this might be too much for you. The thoughts of what you can't have are now staring you dead in the face, taunting you, trying to entice you to come back to the dark side. This may be a behavior that you need to remove from the table, at least until you're strong enough to handle it. Kissing and touching outside the bedroom however, may not be as much of a pressure point.

Kissing and touching are great ways to share and increase intimacy in your relationship. There are a few things to note about kissing and touching, however. Certain parts of the body are off limits, either because they constitute sex (oral), or because they are somewhat of a milder form or variation of sex. They may simply cross the line to where some will feel that if they've gone that far, they may as well go all the way. All genital areas are totally and completely off limits, no exceptions. That means you're not even allowed to use your pinky toe to stroke those areas. Consider those areas, areas with a big red circle and a line across it or covered with a big red X.

Now that that's been said, let's talk about how to use kissing and touching to build intimacy. Use kisses and touches as your form of physical connection, think of it as the celibate version of sex. For many, kissing is a prelude to sex, especially for men. As a celibate person, it is sex. So that means you should take your time with it. Create an environment for kissing, similar to the way you would for sexual intercourse, minus the bed and the relenting of clothes. Vary your style of kisses. Learn how kissing areas such as behind the knee or the small or center of the back can please your partner. Practice techniques such as the anticipation of a kiss, or a touch without the actual physical connection. These can incite passion in the relationship and build upon the intimacy.

Something as small as a touch so light that it only connects with the hair on the skin, can express a great wealth of feelings and emotions. You can gain almost as much pleasure from this as you can from the act of sex. These are just a few examples of how to experience physical intimacy in your relationship while remaining successful in your celibacy. Get creative with your partner and come up with more ways to be intimate beyond sex. Incorporate your physical selves into the relationship while still maintaining your celibacy boundaries.

88: Utilize Trigger Points with <u>Caution</u>

Although sexual intercourse is off the table in a celibate relationship, all forms of physical contact are not. We just talked about using touching and kissing in your relationship as part of your intimacy. We also talked about how to learn some of your partner's trigger points and those areas of their body that incite passion and allows them to receive physical pleasure. For some people they absolutely cannot conceive of not having some form of sexual contact in their romantic relationship. If you need to view touch as a means of sex to help you in your celibacy journey, by all means, please use it. But be careful that you use touch with care.

Be aware, however, that there will be times you will need to limit your use of touch, especially when you or your partner's emotions and/or hormones are so high that resisting sexual intercourse seems nearly impossible. Be sensitive to each other's feelings and don't push it. The goal with utilizing touch and your various trigger points is to allow physical contact in your celibate relationship, not to derail you from your course. Use it to enhance the relationship and to relieve some of the sexual tension that resides within you. But know when to say when.

Establish codes or safe words to let the other person know that things are getting too hot for you and that you need to call it a night. Learn when and how to call it a night and how to retreat to your own separate living quarters. By being cautious with how you use touch and trigger points in your celibate relationship you are that much closer to achieving your goal of being successfully celibate.

89: Develop a New System of <u>Rewards</u>

In various aspects of our lives we are engaged in some sort of rewards program, whether it be at work or in our relationships. It's a part of showing someone that they are appreciated. In relationships the reward system can be used as an award, or as a form of punishment. Sometimes it is used to show your partner how much they're appreciated. We do it because we want to say thank you for something they've done, just for being them or simply because we love them. We also use the rewards system to entice and/or to encourage our partners to come around to our way of thinking or action. Some will use some sort of reward to bring about change in their partner or in their actions. In romantic relationships it's common to see sex used as a reward, as a commodity.

Many people, especially women, use certain aspects of sex as a reward to get their way in the relationship. A mood for lovemaking is set and actions that were previously saved for special occasions are then put into play to effect change. Many men have also played in this game of giving gifts and rewards with sexual intentions being the motive. The opposite has also been known to be true with sex being used as a form of punishment by withholding it from the other.

All, or some, of these things have at one time been a part of a romantic relationship for most people. It comes with the territory of being in a relationship. That's not necessarily a bad thing. What we are saying is that it is something that you need to be aware of, especially in a celibate relationship. If sex has previously been a part of your relationship rewards system, as an award or as a punishment, you need to find other avenues of rewarding and getting your point across. See this as a good thing, as you now have an excuse to find new and exciting ways of providing gratitude and rewards to your partner. It gives you an opportunity to expand your intimacy in yet another way by learning what's important to your partner and implementing that into your relationship reward system.

As an added benefit, when you're married you won't have a need to use sex as a form of punishment to get your way. You have now learned, through your celibate relationship, how to mediate issues in the relationship without factoring sex into the equation. When sex does enter into the relationship, through marriage, you can add sex into the relationship rewards systems as an additional spice to the relationship. When you're in a celibate relationship, you will give up sex for a time (until you're married). But you gain a lot more in the way of being creative in your interaction with one another. This will enhance the sex, when it enters your relationship in its appropriate space and time.

90: Fulfill a <u>Non-Sexual</u> Fantasy

So often many of us fantasize about a variety of things in life that we'd like to do, places we'd like to go, people we'd like to meet or anything else outside of our daily lives that we believe will bring us joy or excitement. But how many of us actually take the time and effort to go after and fulfill those fantasies? Not many. We get caught up in our day-to-day life and put those things on the back burner or completely out of our minds as things that'll never happen to us. Most of us don't even tell our partner about those fantasies for fear they may not understand, or dismiss them as silly. But you might just be surprised to learn that you both share the same fantasy, or similar aspects. It's also another way to bring the two of you closer in the relationship. If you're looking to further your intimacy and trust with your partner, share your fantasies, the secret ones and the not so secret ones.

As you begin to hear the fantasy being told aloud to you, make sure to make a few mental notes of the details. Tuck this away for future use. When you're looking for a way to shower your affection on your partner, call upon this newly gained data and put it into play. Plan it as a surprise occasion where you act out or create one of your partner's fantasies. Based on what the fantasy is, it may be fairly easy to pull off.

For fantasies that are a little more advanced in nature and difficult to pull off, try to fulfill the portions of the fantasy that you can fulfill. Your partner will be ecstatic and floored that you listened to them and made the effort to bring their fantasy to life for them. You may not be able to completely share your physical selves in the form of sexual intercourse while practicing a celibate relationship, but you can share your dreams and desires and magnify them by fulfilling each other's fantasies.

91: Spend a Day Doing <u>Something the Other Likes</u>

Being in a relationship with someone you love can be full of ups and downs. Hopefully there will be many great times with just a few not so great times. Being in any relationship takes work, especially a romantic one. Couples get together for many reasons. Because they have a lot in common, they appreciate the qualities and values the other possesses, and sometimes it's because their partner is strong in areas that they themselves need or want to improve upon in their own life. You've heard the saying "opposites attract." The latter type of couple in the examples just mentioned is usually what one thinks of when they use this phrase. But being different is not a bad thing. Sometimes it's the differences that you share that adds zest to the relationship.

Regardless of where you stand in the arena of life in terms of being an adventurous person, or one who doesn't like to try new things, be open to experiencing something new that you may not have been open to in the past. Be open to navigating new terrains in your relationship. Be supple to trying things that your partner enjoys, even if it's not part of your personal preference. It may be a measure to bring the two of you closer, and yet another way to express the love you share for each other. With the journey of celibacy that the two of you have embarked upon, you want to make sure to not limit yourself in other areas of your relationship beyond the area of sex. One major limitation in a relationship is more than enough.

Pick a day where there is not much going on for either of you and make it about the other person. Spend the day doing something that your partner takes pleasure in, whether you like to do it or not. You might just be surprised to find how much you enjoy that event or activity. The occasion doesn't have to be a big scheme; sometimes it's the smallest things that have the biggest impact. Whether you're the one requesting to share something new with your partner or on the other end of the request being asked to try something new, be open to the experience.

Have you heard the sentiment, don't block someone's blessing? What that means is that sometimes by one person doing something for someone else, a blessing has been set up for him or her through that particular act of kindness. Not knowing that there is a blessing waiting for them, that person attempts to do something nice for you, just because. Say for whatever reason, you decline to allow them to do this for you. By your refusal, you may have inadvertently blocked a blessing that was meant for them, through their act of kindness to you. Be careful not to block the blessings of others or steal their joy by not allowing them to show you their love in this fashion.

I remember once being in a relationship with someone where this occurred. He came to pick me up to take me out. There was a new restaurant that he found and wanted to share with me. He was so excited because he knew how much I would like this place and he simply wanted to please me. For whatever reason, that night I was just not in the mood for trying new things and asked him to take me someplace I was more familiar with. He was disappointed but he acquiesced and took me elsewhere. I finally went to this restaurant a year or two after we were no longer seeing each other. And he was right; I did really like it. I can't tell you how disappointed I was with myself at that moment. Here was this man who I cared about and who cared about me, trying to share something he liked with me and how oblivious I was to his attempt and affection toward me. Because I chose to be wrapped in selfishness, I missed a great opportunity to grow the relationship.

During this time, we were sexually involved so I could have attempted to try and make it up to him through sex. As a celibate couple sex is not an option to attempt to appease hurt feelings. Instead, how about trying to open yourself up to your partner a bit more and take the time to spend the day, half a day, or even just a few hours showing them how much you care about them by doing something that they like. If you're already doing it, continue on as you are definitely on the right path of having a successfully celibate relationship. If you're not, give it a try!

92: <u>Create</u> a Token of Love

A token of love is a great way to remind your partner that they are loved and appreciated by you. It's also a symbol of the commitment that the two of you have made to be celibate until your wedding night. When a couple becomes engaged to be married, a ring is usually presented to the woman to wear. This ring tells her your intentions toward her; it's a promise to marry. It tells the rest of the world that she is loved and has been chosen to be the bride of the man who loves her. In most wedding ceremonies there is a second ring presented to the woman to seal the deal. In double ring ceremonies, both participants are presented with a wedding ring to show that that person is no longer available to become romantically involved with any other person.

One can look at their ring and gain a sense of comfort from its meaning. The ring is also a visual reminder to the wearer of what they have: the other person, a commitment. When temptation introduces itself, the ring can speak in place of your partner telling you not to jeopardize what you already have at home. It's amazing how something so small can do so much! In a celibate relationship, a token of love does the exact same thing. It reminds you of why you're being celibate, of what's at stake if you break your vow.

A token of love can be anything, big or small, expensive or inexpensive. Whatever it is, allow it to be from the heart. Allow it to be something that you two can share together. Something that you can give each other to show that you are both in this committed celibate relationship together. Let it be a reminder that you can carry around with you in the same manner that a married person wears their wedding ring. It can be a piece of jewelry, but it doesn't have to be. It can be something that fits in a wallet, hangs from the rearview mirror of your car, or attaches to a key chain. Just make sure that it has meaning for you both and that it'll remind you of your commitment to each other to travel down this road of celibacy together.

93: <u>Exercise</u> Together

Exercise is another part of life. Many people partake in it and many don't. The thing about exercise is that it is a necessity, whether we realize it or not. It is a means to help you maintain your health physically as well as mentally and emotionally. Physically it can help your body function better and even help stave off or help in controlling a variety of diseases. Exercise has been proven to improve one's mood, reduce stress and increase energy, not to mention its weight loss properties. When you're in a celibate relationship you will more than likely experience an increase of stress and tension because you don't have the physical release through sexual intercourse. Therefore, you need to find another physical outlet. Let that outlet be exercise and let it be something that the two of you do as a couple.

If neither of you like to exercise, find a creative way to accomplish it. Play a game of Frisbee®, volleyball, go swimming or any other activity that gets you moving. Think of games that you played in childhood and incorporate those into your routine to make it fun and different. Encourage each other to become or to stay active. By doing so you are helping your partner to be healthy. You're also bringing another avenue of strength to the relationship in the way of motivation. If your partner despises exercise and would rather do anything else but exercise, be there to encourage them and to accentuate the positives of exercise. Help convince them of the need to begin a routine and work it out with them. By providing support, you have just given them further confidence in you and the relationship as a whole. You're showing your commitment to them and to the relationship.

Whether in a celibate or non-celibate relationship, it's important to know that you can count on your partner to encourage you and to look out for your best interests. But having it in a celibate relationship tends to have a deeper impact because there are limitations and sacrifices placed on the celibate relationship, which aren't present in a sexual relationship. It gives the celibate relationship a greater sense of security. It's easy to say that you are supportive of your partner. To show it is a whole other thing. Use exercise to help you say something in a big way.

94: <u>Learn</u> Together

Learning a new hobby or taking a class with your partner can be a great way to better communicate with them. Each of us has our own way of learning, whether it is hands-on, through auditory methods, individual study or a combination of these techniques or other methods. When you spend time learning together, you witness how your partner best receives and translates concepts. In addition to processing information, you see how they respond positively and negatively, through this experience, in a way that is different from their responses to relationship matters.

Throughout this book we talk about giving it (whatever "it" is) to a person right, giving them information in a loving and respectful manner that they can embrace and best absorb. Taking a class together or learning something new can present a good example of the manner of style in which your partner best receives new things. It provides you with the best framework in which to express your message, to give it to them right. In addition to witnessing how your partner best learns and receives information, you've also gained a new skill, hobby, et cetera and your relationship will have grown even more so by adding another thing that the two of you can share together.

95: Cook <u>Together</u>

Food can have different impacts on people and can be used in areas beyond satisfying hunger. It can serve as a method of expression or it can quietly teach a person something new about him or herself, or even someone else. It can be a source of emotional discomfort or a means of accomplishing a goal. People have different relationships with food. Some they are aware of and some they are not. Because food is something that is critical to life and something that we simply cannot live without, it takes on a much larger dynamic than most people would imagine or admit to.

So how does food fit into the circumference of being in a celibate relationship? Let me explain. Food itself is not so much an ingredient in the celibate relationship. It's how it is used in the process of preparation and the small insights into your partner's psyche and personality that are unleashed, that benefit the celibate relationship. Because food is intimate in the way that it travels inside the body, what is done to prepare it for its journey gives you insight to how your partner thinks of their physical and mental self. Experiencing these clues and revelations during the cooking process, is information that can be used to draw the two of you closer together and to share a deeper level of intimacy.

I'll give you an example. I thoroughly enjoy cooking. For me it's another way to tinker with my creativity. If you give me a recipe to follow, one of two things will happen. I will follow it and add my own touches to it, or I will follow it completely, and it will be off. Now it's not to say that I can't follow a recipe as written, because I can. But it's because cooking gives me a chance to use my imagination and I want to make sure that I don't let the opportunity pass me by. Usually, the more creative I am in my cooking, the less chance I have to be creative in other areas of my life because of stress or life's pressures or obligations.

Because I have to cook to eat, I find the freedom to just let go and see what my mind creates. Rarely will I cook the same dish twice and have it taste exactly the same. This is because I cook by feeling. When I am preparing a meal, I go to my spice rack and stand there for a moment. I look at the various spices and see what speaks to me. Based on how I'm feeling at that time, it will determine what will go in the dish, hence the reason my food never tastes exactly the same each time I make it. If my confidence is high, my food has enormous flavor and is delectable. If my mood is low or my comfort level is waning, my food isn't as tasty as it could be. I then find myself second-guessing the ingredients during the process, and afterward while eating. These are feelings that I may not share with my partner openly, but things that they can pickup through spending time cooking with me.

By cooking together you become more in tune to how your partner is feeling on a day-to-day basis. By witnessing your partner's unconscious cooking cues while cooking together, you are presented with a golden opportunity to learn more about them and how they think and what they are feeling. Some of the same personality cues you would pick up on during sexual intercourse can be exposed during the cooking process. You can then take what you have learned during cooking together and apply it to other aspects of your relationship and your partner's communication style. You have just gained another level of intimacy and knowing each other in a manner that sexual intercourse may or may not have offered the two of you.

96: <u>Do</u> a Task That the Other Hates

There are so many things that we each need to do on a daily or weekly basis to live in society. Some things we like to do, some we are okay with and some we simply despise for whatever reason. Regardless of our feelings toward these things, we still need to do them to facilitate smoother operations in our daily lives. Imagine coming home or starting your day and finding that your partner has taken the liberty of taking one of those things off your plate and accomplishing it so you don't have to. It can be something small like putting the laundry away. I have no issue with washing and folding laundry, but I hate putting it away. So much so that I have a bad habit of leaving it folded on the washer and dryer, even though it will only take me a few steps to put it away. Imagine how I would feel to have the man I was in a relationship with come over, see the clothes and put them up for me. That would speak volumes of his feelings for me and make me appreciate him that much more. For him, putting away the laundry could be a small thing. For me, it's a big thing.

But imagine that they hate it as much as you do, but they did it anyway because they wanted to put a smile on your face. Imagine how that would feel to be on the receiving end of such a grand gesture. Imagine how it would feel to be on the giving end of the task and to see the surprise and gratitude of your partner. Chances are, the effort expended to complete the task was not so great. Even if it was, you've gained so much more in return by the response from your partner. You've just found yet another way, outside of the bedroom, to express your love and admiration to the person that you are in a relationship with. Being celibate isn't just about abstaining from sex. It is also about finding different and creative ways to connect to your partner and to express your love to and for them. Take a moment and do something that your partner hates, just because. Watch how much better it makes you both feel for having done it.

97: <u>Set Goals</u>, Celebrate When Achieved, Set New Ones

As a couple, it is important to be on the same page with one another. In order for your relationship to be fulfilling to both of you, you need to communicate your wants, needs and the goals that you'd each like to accomplish in the relationship. When the two of you chose to become a celibate couple, that was a goal that you agreed upon and began working toward together. This is one of the first steps in having a successful celibate relationship. Throughout this section we've provided you with a number of ways to help increase the intimacy and further build trust and respect in the relationship. You now have many great building blocks to pave the road to a wonderful relationship that honors God, your souls and your bodies.

Keep that momentum going by challenging yourselves to be even better by setting goals. The goals can be individual or combined. They are there to keep the relationship moving forward and to help prevent it from becoming stagnant. Goals are also there to help keep you grounded in your beliefs and moving in a forward direction. When you have taken steps to bring your goals to fruition, you are less likely to deviate from the plan. If there are no goals to strive for, you are just free flowing and it becomes much easier to slack off in other areas of your life.

By setting goals, you have something to look forward to. You have a preplanned celebration waiting for you at the end. You've set a goal of celibacy and you're working on it daily. At some point in the relationship you decide to get married and your celibacy ends. What is the next goal that the two of you will work toward together? Will it be having kids, buying a house, returning to school, getting a better job? Will your goals be the same? How do you know if you're not setting them now? Once you begin setting goals together, you may find that your goals differ. If this is the case, it's better to know sooner rather than later so you can begin to work on getting on the same page now for smoother sailing later on.

Set small, medium and larger goals. Set short-term and long-term goals. When you've reached a goal, celebrate and check it off your list. Rejoice in the comfort that you are building your future together and that you've succeeded in working together either in your plan or in encouraging the other to meet their goal. After you've celebrated, set new goals to work on and watch how much stronger your relationship has become. On those days when you question whether you'll continue to be celibate until the end, look back at the other goals in the relationship that you have set, accomplished and celebrated and let them fuel you on in your celibacy walk.

98: <u>Attend Church</u> Together

For many people attending church is part of their Christian walk. They gain strength from the uplifting sermons and songs sung by the choir. They kneel at the altar, throw themselves on the mercy of God and cast their cares upon Him. They delight in partaking of the symbolic blood and wine that represents the sacrifice that Jesus has made for us all. Witnessing other Christians and what God has done for them in their lives serves as an encouragement to others who are struggling with a variety and multitude of issues and problems.

For many, church is seen as more than just a sanctuary. It is a spiritual hospital to go to heal their soul. Some feel closer to God in their church. As we all know, God is everywhere, everywhere that we are. But for some, because the building is a physical representation of His house, it is a great comfort for many to be there. For some it is like going home. Church can be seen as the believers' place of security.

On the other hand, there are many people who believe in God deeply within themselves. For some, the God that lives within them is more than enough and they feel no need to go to a physical structure to draw closer to Him. All they have to do is look inside his or her self to get closer to Him, to feel Him. Many of these people don't feel the need to attend a church service on a regular basis. Lots of these people don't require the hearing of God's words from a minister; they have a Bible and can read the Word for themselves. Some fear that man will place his interpretation on the Word and shape it to fit the needs of their self or some other hidden agenda. These people believe in God and operate their lives in the best manner that they believe in, based on their personal beliefs, values and what they've read in the Bible.

If you're in a celibate relationship with someone, based on the biblical principles of waiting until marriage to consummate the relationship, you need to make sure that you are both also on the same page when it comes to your belief system and how each of you operates in it. Part of that belief system should include attending church, as this is where you can gain strength in maintaining your celibacy through the hearing of the Word of God.

Not forsaking or neglecting to assemble together [as believers], as is the habit of some people, but admonishing (warning, urging, and encouraging) one another, and all the more faithfully as you see the day approaching.

–Hebrews 10:25 (AMP)

If you're in a relationship, then you should be attending church with your significant other. Imagine that the two of you are planning on taking a trip or even planning a life together and you decide to take two different paths to get there. When you reach your final destination, how likely is that you'll both still be on the same agenda? While you each took separate paths to the same destination, the journey that you each traveled to get there was different.

So now what you thought was the same, has been altered. Can you both continue on together with an altered picture that doesn't look the same to both of you? Yes, you probably can. But chances are, because your journeys were different, your visions have likely shifted as well and you will experience more differences in the future. This can cause problems that needn't have been there had you been traveling on the same path from the beginning. Now view the previous scenario from the stance of attending church together. One of you believes in attending church and one of you does not, or you each attend church but belong to two different churches.

In each church, the minister is there to feed their flock. Each minister will differ from the next in the messages they deliver to their flock. Two ministers can deliver the same sermon on the same subject but with a different spin. The differences can be minimal or they can be great, great enough to impact the relationship. When you're in a celibate relationship following the will of God, you are a bit more vulnerable because you are going against the devil. Don't make things any harder for yourselves by creating a potential area of contention that doesn't need to be there. If you are to grow together as a successful celibate couple you need to receive your food and meals from the same source, by attending the same church together.

99: Pray <u>Together</u>

Throughout this section we've talked about several ways to increase and build the intimacy in a celibate relationship. By far, the greatest path to constructing intimacy is through sharing a prayer life together. Individual prayer is the one opportunity to experience the truest form of one's self. This is the time when a person is most vulnerable as they open up their spirit and pour out their petitions, gratitude and love to God, their Lord and Savior. People participate in corporate prayer in church, at family dinners and during any number of special occasions when they express their wishes and desires for others near and far.

But personal prayer is your time to present your own wants, needs and desires to God, without the listening ears of others or the fear of judgment of what you're requesting or discussing with God. It is a sacred time between you and God. As a celibate couple, you are not sharing your internal bodies but you can share your next most precious intimacy, the intimacy of personal prayer through praying together.

Praying together as a couple is not something that has to or even should be done on every occasion that prayer takes place. You still need your individual time alone with God to build your personal relationship with Him. Do not forsake alone time with God. It is needed for each of us to grow and to become better people and to learn the plans that God has for our life. Designate a portion of your prayer life to time alone in prayer with your partner. This is a time for the two of you to join as one and to enter into prayer on one accord with a singular petition. You may not be at the same level of maturity in your Christian walk but through praying together, you can certainly begin to lessen the gap of where you both stand.

Praying together can bring you two to a level place in prayer because you are drawing on the strength of each other and you are going before God as one. You are saying to God that you desire to be on level ground spiritually. By taking the action to actually pray as one, it gives validity to your words and shows God the intensity of your desire to be equally yoked in your Christian and celibate walk. As a celibate couple, you may not be joining yourself together physically but you are by no means limited in joining yourselves together in other areas of great importance in your life.

There are other benefits to praying together, an important one being that it draws God into the midst of your presence, into the midst of your intimate prayer time together. It takes your level of intimacy to a height that you can't reach together otherwise, not even through the act of sex. It also increases the power of your petition to Him because you are turning to Him to meet your needs. It's like adding fuel to your prayers.

Imagine driving in a car that already has a great deal of power to get you to high speeds with minimal time lapse or effort. This is like praying alone. Then you depress the turbo button (begin praying together), and instantly from the second you put your foot to the pedal you're moving at lightning speed to your final destination. This is what praying together will do for your combined petition. It will skyrocket the prayers from your hearts to the ears of God and into action.

Again I tell you, if two of you on earth agree (harmonize together, make a symphony together) about whatever [anything and everything] they may ask, it will come to pass and be done for them by My Father in heaven. For wherever two or three are gathered (drawn together as My followers) in (into) My name, there I AM in the midst of them.

–Matthew 18:19-20 (AMP)

Don't forsake the power of praying together. It can be one of your strongest weapons in the war of maintaining your celibacy.

Sexual intercourse is part of romantic relationships, but for a time. Health, emotional issues, distance and other factors may very well become a hindrance to a couple connecting sexually during some part of their overall relationship. Prayer, however, has no limitations and no boundaries. It can intertwine a couple together even more so than sex can. Making praying together a part of your celibate relationship is a crucial step in building a foundation that can't easily be shaken or broken.

100: Embrace the Less Loved Things about <u>Your Partner</u>

At this point in the relationship you've probably learned many things about each other, good and bad. If you've followed the ways outlined in this book to learn more about each other, there are certainly some things you now know that you didn't know before beginning this journey of celibacy. But they are all things that make your partner who they are. All of their traits and quirks, good and bad, are necessary for them to be a whole person. The areas of their personality that are less than favorable to you may be an area within yourself that you have an issue with and seeing it in your partner just magnifies it in you. Or it can be something that is just a pet peeve to you.

Whatever it is, use it to help you both grow individually and/or as a couple. If you are the only one with the issue, there may be something within yourself that you need to look at and deal with. It could be a test for you to improve in that area. View it as such and get to work. If it's an area that impacts and/or bothers many others, then take it as an opportunity to address it with your partner, as it may be a test for them to work on. It may be a non-entity that your partner is not even aware of and may require you to shine light on it in order for them to become aware of it. Or, it just may be a part of who they are and they're not going to change. Your goal here is not to try and change each other, but to love and embrace every part of each other. It is not only for the relationship and your own mental well being, it is also pleasing to God.

I THEREFORE, the prisoner for the Lord, appeal to and beg you to walk (lead a life) worthy of the [divine] calling to which you have been called [with behavior that is a credit to the summons to God's service, Living as becomes you] with complete lowliness of mind (humility) and meekness (unselfishness, gentleness, mildness), with patience, bearing with one another and making allowances because you love one another. Be eager and strive earnestly to guard and keep the harmony and oneness of [and produced by] the Spirit in the binding power of peace.

–Ephesians 4:1-3 (AMP)

If this is the case, accept it as a gift designed to help you communicate better with one another. A gift that teaches you how to deal with an issue using the love that you share for each other; where you learn to agree to disagree, without it causing havoc in the relationship. Take it as a gift of growth in the area of maturity. If you can view it in this manner, it will help you not to allow this to become an issue during the less than happy or difficult times of your celibate relationship.

Here's where embracing your partner's less loved habits can differ and benefit you in a way that it may not do as much so in a sexual relationship. In a sexual relationship if the sex is really good, you can use sex as somewhat of a temporary salve to lessen your irritation of your partner's habits that don't line up with your good side. But when there is no sex in the relationship and you become irritated from a variety of things, including lack of sex, those little things become magnified. The sexual salve that you used in the past is no longer viable and your irritation has a greater sense of heightening. If you stay in this mood, your mind can begin to play tricks on you and color your emotions in a negative way. This is not necessarily a bad thing, but a human thing.

Knowing that this could happen, learning to embrace those things about your partner that you don't care so much for, prevents the need to have a salve or band-aid. When, and if the irritation should arise, you already have a plan of attack to combat those negative thoughts without endangering your relationship or your celibacy. When you control those negative thoughts, you are that much stronger in your walk of celibacy.

If on the other hand, you're not prepared to deal with them, small things can seem much bigger than they are and cause you to question things that don't need to be questioned. The door has then been opened to doubt and for Satan to add fuel to the fire and make you begin to question your entire walk. Be the master of your fate in your celibacy walk. Put safe guards in place to keep you moving forward in your celibacy journey.

101: Spend Time Getting to <u>Know the Family/Friends</u> of Your Partner

While you're spending time and effort putting in the work to create a strong, healthy and happy celibate relationship with your partner, be sure to include those who are of value to your partner. By doing so, you accomplish two goals. First, by drawing closer to your partner's family and friends, you are drawing closer to your partner by showing them that those who are important to him or her are also important to you. You are letting them know that you support those connections and relationships and understand that they are a part of your partner and part of what makes them who they are. You are setting a comfortable environment for your partner that says he or she does not have to choose between you and their family and friends, but that you all can and do coexist together.

Secondly, getting to know your partner's family and friends allows you to see who is influencing your partner and in what manner. If there is someone new in the mix and there is a shift that suddenly appears in your partner or in the relationship, you now know where that shift is coming from. By having this knowledge, you now have a starting point to address with your partner and help you both get back on the path to success. The opposite is also true as you can identify an ally to help encourage your partner when you need help in encouraging them.

As you walk together on this journey of celibacy or in your relationship as a whole, sometimes you will be all that your partner needs to move forward. At other times it will take an army to do the job. In Section I of this book we talked about forming an army to help see you through to the end of your celibacy walk. Each of you should have your own army in place that you can turn to for support. Utilize your army. Know the army of each other. You won't necessarily need to use your partner's army, but it's good to know that they're there and who they are, should you need to make use of their support. Knowing the army (family and friends) of your partner is but another way to love your partner and to add another brick in the road to you both successfully completing your walk of celibacy!

* * * * *

Congratulations! You've done it! You've gone through each of the steps and now know what it takes to be successfully celibate. You now understand that celibacy is about more than just abstaining from sex. You now see and appreciate the effects that sex has on your heart, mind, soul and your body. With this new knowledge, you are equipped to make better choices that not only honor all the parts that makes you a whole person, but also honors the word of God in this area of your life. During your journey you've learned to lean and rely on God in ways that you previously hadn't. As a result, you now have a much stronger and fulfilling relationship with Him.

In addition to learning what it takes to be a solo celibate adult, you've also learned with it is like being a celibate female, a celibate male and a celibate couple. If you've implemented the many tools found within the pages of this book, you now have a much stronger celibate relationship than you would have had, had you not read this book. Tools that have shown you how to increase the intimacy, respect and overall trust in your celibate relationship. You've even gained a few pointers on having a physical relationship that still preserves your vow of saving sex until marriage.

Where ever you are on your celibacy walk from contemplating beginning the journey, at the start, mid way through or on the verge of ending it as you are now entering into the next phase of your life as a married couple, the things that you've learned in these pages have altered and shaped your life for the better. You are a new and improved creation who understands their value to God, to themselves, to others and to the world as a whole! You have confidence soaring in you like never before because you have undertaken or have accomplished a great and difficult feat and have come out sparkling as a diamond!

Take the things that you've learned about yourself and communicating with others and apply them to other areas of your life and see if you're not better for them! I pray this work has been a good source of information, comfort and encouragement to you in your walk of celibacy. As you continue to grow as a person and in your life overall, share with others the things that you have learned on this path.

Don't take what you've learned here and hoard it to yourself. Share it with others and be the example to them whether it is in the realm of celibacy or in life itself by the way that you communicate and treat people. If you were blessed by these words, be a blessing to others. Imagine if I had kept this wonderful gift of living successfully in celibacy, that God has shared with me, to myself. How would that have impacted you in not having this book to help support you in your walk? You could still be successful in your journey, you certainly can be. But you wouldn't have had the benefit of learning from some of my pitfalls, which you can now avoid because you have this word.

Remember early on and throughout the book we talked about gathering your survival words and creating a journal? Well this is an area where those items come in to play. Use them to help you develop your own testimony to share with someone else that is also going through the walk of celibacy. Be the encouragement to them. Iron sharpens iron.

During the writing of this book I hit a few roadblocks and wanted to just stop where I was. In those times, God reminded me that I was not just writing this book for my own benefit. Although many of the words in these pages encourage and keep *me* on the path, they were not designed solely for my benefit, but also for *your* benefit. God would remind me that this work is not about me. It's about *you*.

Therefore, I was not allowed to quit and had to push on to deliver these words to you. Now it's your turn to pass them on to the next person on the path. This is how we will create *The Celibacy Movement*, one person at a time helping someone else to be successfully celibate. Please continue the chain and we will reach our goal of 1 million people living successfully celibate!

P. S. Don't forget to sign your celibacy pledge.

Covenant Pledge of Celibacy for Singles

I, _____, do solemnly pledge to enter into covenant with You my Heavenly Father, Jesus Christ, on this _____ day of the month of _ _____ in the year of _____, to walk in celibacy and Christian love until the day that I wed in holy matrimony.

I pledge to not engage in any sexual intercourse with anyone other than my spouse who is sent by You, God. I pledge to turn to You, my Lord when times get rough and my footing in this journey lacks stability.

I pledge to seek You, Lord, first in action through prayer and reading of Your Word when my strength is weaning.

I pledge to work on my relationship with You and with myself to keep both You and my commitment to this journey as my first priority, which in turn will provide me strength and solace down this path.

I pledge that if I shall fail in this task that I will come to You and ask for Your forgiveness. I pledge that once You have forgiven me, I too shall forgive myself and continue on my journey.

I pledge that I will not wallow in past failures, but learn from them to help guide me when I'm faced with similar or more aggressive tests.

I pledge to not challenge You or myself through entering into situations that can lead me to a destination that is not in line with this pledge. This is my pledge!

_____

(Signature of Person Entering Pledge)

_____

(Name of Person Entering Pledge)

_____

(Witness of Person Entering Pledge)

About the Author

So just a brief word about why I'm writing this book. In my late teens to early 20s I thought I was just too cute. I was certainly smelling myself! My first year of college was a little wild. After that I joined the military, settled down quite a bit and swore off men for awhile, just to get back in touch with me. Then it started up again when I read *How Stella Got Her Groove Back,* the bestseller novel by Terry McMillan. So I went traipsing off to Jamaica in search of a Winston of my own! Like they say what happens in Vegas stays in Vegas, well the same holds true for Jamaica! I was there alone, but had not a want for an ounce of company, and that's all I'll say about that excursion.

During this time, things began to change. Men were attracted to me and my resume was in check with a college degree, a nice car, a good job and traveling wherever and whenever I wanted to. I was a hot commodity; at least that's how I saw myself! I had my pick from an older guy who owned multiple houses, an attractive maintenance man with his own company, expensive cars and any woman he wanted and the man who I had at once deemed, the love of my life. I had these three men in rotation. When I didn't get what I wanted from one, I'd go to the next.

I was sinning and claiming to be a Christian while sitting up in church on Sunday mornings and Wednesday evenings and spending many nights in the bed of one of my lovers. Not a good look for a female, I know! One of my lovers even likened my style of encounters to that of a dude's in the way that I went from one to the other and abruptly left when the events of the night were over, not to awaken in the bed of any!

As I was doing my dirt and attending church, God began to move in my life and convict me of my wrongdoings and promiscuous behavior. At first it would start with a well-placed word in my Pastor's sermons to full-blown sermons about not having sex outside of marriage. If that wasn't bad enough, the enjoyment that I had once received from my rendezvous was no longer appealing to me or even whetting my whistle. Nothing had changed about the acts or the techniques or the touches that these men used to excite me. If anything, they had become more skilled at reading my body and utilizing their knowledge to its fullest extent.

What *did* change was the way I felt about being with the men I was with, and the way I felt about myself. It had even gotten to the point where somewhere during the act I would emotionally and spiritually get up and leave the room. There was an occasion or two when my partner would have to ask me if I was still there with him or where it was that I had gone to because he too had felt the departure. My spirit would no longer allow me to abuse my body in that manner. But still, I didn't always listen and I went back for more of the same. I'd stop for a bit, but back I would go.

The final straw was immediately following sex, while still lying in his bed, I would begin to cry and become depressed because I had yet again disappointed and betrayed God and His will for my life. I've got to tell you, it only takes a time or two of weeping in a man's bed following sex, for him to say, "I'm good!" when you call him again. No man's ego wants to believe that having sex with him is depressing and known to cause bouts of crying fits.

Unless you're a fool, you're only going to continue to stick your hand in the fire so many times before you finally give up the effort and move on. I'd like to think that I'm no fool, but it did take me awhile to get that I shouldn't have been having sex outside of marriage. I no longer achieved joy and pleasure from having sex outside of marriage. It was simply that my soul had left the building!

Finally giving in and turning my will over to God, and living a life of celibacy, was the only solace that I was able to find. Through sermons, conversations with God (prayer), reading the Bible and the abandonment of my spirit during the act, I acquiesced. I had done what God had asked of me. I believed it was my time for rest, for me to have peace. At least that's where I thought it had ended. But just as God would not let up on me about not having sex outside of marriage, He would not let up on me about speaking out on this subject and helping others through this journey by sharing my testimony.

I don't provide my background here for you as means of pumping myself up.

My past behavior does not show me in the most favorable light. I do it to let you know that I understand the power and the desire that resides in one with a healthy sexual
appetite. I tell you these things because I know how hard it is to go from one extreme to the next, and that it is possible to change for the better.

I also tell you these things so you can better understand the struggles and the withdrawals that one can go through in this journey. So that you know that my words ring true when I say you can succeed in this walk. Know that when I tell you stories in this book, I speak from my real life emotions and my real life experiences. I speak to encourage and to strengthen you to surpass whatever you come up against in this celibacy walk. Finally, I write this book as an attempt to be obedient to my Father, Jesus Christ, who has instructed me to do so.

My Walk of Celibacy

So, of course, I'm sure you'd like to know where I'm at with my walk (as I talk to you about *your* walk). I am currently one year into my most recent vow of celibacy. The first time was for one year. The second was for two years. My third was six and two (I had a minor hiccup in between years six and seven, even though I like to think that that doesn't count, it does). Following that were two small breaks and now my current vow of just over one year in counting. My most recent slip was an attempt of fulfilling a fantasy about someone that I've known for years.

The lessons that I learned are that if you are not constant and vigilant in pursing your goal of celibacy through every phase of your singlehood, you open the door for havoc to come in and take the reins and to throw you off your chosen course. No matter how much time you have under your belt of celibacy, you must still work the steps and be mindful about your mission on a daily basis. I've also learned that sometimes a fantasy needs to remain a fantasy. You can't expect skyrockets when you clearly and willingly go against God's will, and your own will for your life. It just doesn't work that way.

So as you can see, even with all the practice that I've had, even I still make mistakes. Even I need to be attentive about maintaining my celibacy and practicing the things I lay out here in this book on a daily basis. The key is to not allow it to remain a mistake, but to start again. Yes, there will be times that you will fail. Don't focus on the failure. Focus on the fact that you were able to maintain your celibacy as long as you did. Focus on the fact that you have progressed in your celibacy walk.

There were some temptations that used to trip you up, that now, no longer do. Celebrate those successes and thank God for being able to maintain. Stay vigilant. Ask Him for forgiveness, learn from your errors and keep it movin'! I pray this work is encouraging to you and helpful in *Your Successful Walk of Celibacy*!

Be Blessed!

References

Atkins-Campbell, Erica/Atkins-Campbell Trecina "Tina" (performed by Mary Mary). "I Try." INCREDIBLE. Columbia, 2007. CD.

Atkins-Campbell, Erica/Atkins-Campbell Trecina "Tina" (performed by Mary Mary). "If I Fall." INCREDIBLE (hidden track #22). Columbia, 2007. CD.

Bagnerise, Carla. 2005, "Celibacy Equals=Life: About the Ultimate Personal Relationship." AuthorHouse.

Barnes, S./Bridges, C./Oliver, J.C./Range of Stargate/T-Pain (performed by Ludacris). "One More Drink." THEATRE OF THE MIND. DTP, Def Jam, 2008. CD.

BBC Worldwide. 2005-Present. ABC. "Dancing With The Stars."

Bond, Kevin (performed by Yolanda Adams). "In The Midst Of It All." MOUNTAIN HIGH... VALLEY LOW. Elektra, 1999. CD.

Byrne, Rhonda. 2006, "The Secret" Atria Books/Beyond Words

Chapman, Gary. 2004. "The Five Love Languages of God: How to Feel and Reflect Divine Love." Northfield Publishing

Chapman, Gary. 2004, "The Five Love Languages for Singles." Northfield Publishing

Cozzens, Donald B. 2006. "Freeing Celibacy." Liturgical Press.

Eggerichs, Emerson. 2004, "Love & Respect: The Love She Most Desires; The Respect He Desperately Needs. Thomas Nelson.

Thomas, Kathern Ann. 2004, "Celebrating Celibacy." AuthorHouse.

Esquivel, Laura. (1992). Alfonso Arau. "Like Water For Chocolate."

George, Elizabeth (2004) "A Wife After God's Own Heart: 12 Things That Really Matter in Your Marriage." Harvest House Publishers.

Jr. Dollar, Dr. Creflo A. 2000, "Lord Teach Me How To Love: Learning from the Ultimate Example." Harrison House.

McMickle, Marvin A./Butts, Calvin O. 2003.,"Before We Say I Do: 7 Steps to a

Healthy Marriage." Judson Press.

Mitchell, F.S. 2006, "Celebrating Celibacy." Xulon Press

Morris, Marilyn. 1995, "Abstinence - The New Sexual Revolution." Charles River Publishing Company.

Napier, Kristine. 1996, "The Power of Abstinence." Avon Books.

Peace, Martha. 1999, "The Excellent Wife: A Biblical Perspective." Focus Publishing.

Pearl, Debi. 2004, "Created to Be His Help Meet: Discover How God Can Make Your Marriage Glorious." Joy Ministries.

Sipe, A.W. Richard. 1996, "Celibacy: A Way of Loving, Living, and Serving." Liguori Publications.

Warren, Rick. 2002, "The Purpose Driven Life." Zondervan

Wiggins, R (performed by Tony! Toni! Tone!). "I Couldn't Keep It To Myself." SONS OF SOUL. Wing/Mercury, 1993. CD

Williams, Donna Marie. 1999, "Sensual Celibacy: The Sexy Woman's Guide to Using Abstinence for Recharging Your Spirit, Discovering Your Passions, Achieving Greater Intimacy in Your Next Relationship." Touchstone.

www.ingramcontent.com/pod-product-compliance
Lightning Source LLC
Chambersburg PA
CBHW081212020426
42331CB00012B/2999